A Study of Blackbirds

A Study of Blackbirds

BY D. W. SNOW

Illustrated by Robert Gillmor

BRITISH MUSEUM (NATURAL HISTORY)

© D. W. Snow 1988
First published 1958
Second edition 1988
British Museum (Natural History)
Cromwell Road
London
SW7 5BD
Cataloguing in publication data

Snow, David
  A study of blackbirds – 2nd ed.
  1. Blackbirds
  I. Title
  598.8'42   QL696.P2475

  ISBN 0-565-01021-2

CONTENTS

L'observateur se promenant le long de pelouses et bosquets apprend à connaître les territoires et leurs habitants; il s'arrête pour voir vivre le monde des merles et participe à ses espoirs, ses réussites, ses échecs.

ELISABETH MEUGENS

[The observer walking the length and breadth of the lawns and thickets gets to know the different territories and their inhabitants; he stops to see how the world of the blackbirds lives and to share its hopes, its successes and its failures.]

ILLUSTRATIONS

PREFACE TO THE SECOND EDITION

It is now nearly 30 years since the first edition of this book was published, and it has been out of print for some time. Meanwhile a number of new and interesting things have been found out about Blackbirds. I have not, however, altered the text; my account was not meant to be a monograph, giving everything that is known about Blackbirds, but was based almost entirely on the small Blackbird population living in and around the Botanic Garden at Oxford. Nevertheless it may be of interest to mention a few of the more outstanding points on which new light has been thrown in recent years. They are dealt with in a postscript (page 191).

I am very grateful to George Allen & Unwin for readily allowing the British Museum (Natural History) to re-issue the book unaltered, and to Robert Gillmor for agreeing to the re-use of his illustrations and for designing a new cover. Following the fortunes of any population of small birds month after month demands a great deal of time. I had fewer other commitments 35 years ago than I have now; but even so, I should never have been able to devote so much time to Blackbirds without the considerable degree of freedom allowed me by the late David Lack, Director of the Edward Grey Institute. His unrivalled *Life of the Robin* encouraged me to attempt something similar for the Blackbird, and I dedicate this second edition to his memory.

——— I ———

Introduction

I BEGAN watching blackbirds in January 1953, mainly because they were common and conspicuous in the Oxford Botanic Garden, on which I looked down from my window at the Edward Grey Institute. Then I trapped and colour-ringed some of them, so that I began to know them individually, and before long I was devoting most of the time that I could spare to a study of their behaviour, their population changes, and such other aspects of their biology as could be studied in the field, by simple techniques. In the course of four years I was able to collect information on nearly a hundred colour-ringed birds of each sex living in or near the Botanic Garden, and of these, the histories of about forty birds of each sex were recorded in some detail. An account of this local population forms the core of this book.

The Botanic Garden at Oxford, the oldest in the country, is comparatively small. Four seventeenth-century walls surround a square of a little over three acres containing lawns, paths and flower-beds, the whole well planted with trees and shrubs. The present garden extends to about twice the area of the original walled square, the newer part beyond the wall being less formal than the rest, with rough grass, thick bushes and a small pond that is much used as a bathing place by the garden birds. One side of the garden is bounded by the River Cherwell, beyond which lie the garden and playing field of Magdalen College School. Along part of the opposite side the garden abuts on the open fields of Christ Church Meadow, while a part adjoins Merton College, and on the remaining side it is bordered by the buildings of the Bureau of Animal Population, Edward Grey Institute and Magdalen College Estate Office (the old Herbarium), with the traffic-filled High Street beyond.

These Botanic Garden blackbirds thus live in a habitat which is urban at one end and almost rural at the other. For the observer however the most important point is that it is a public place, open for most of the day and tended by a staff of gardeners. From living constantly close to human beings who do not interfere with them, the blackbirds become very tame, and much of their behaviour can be watched at close quarters. In woodland near Oxford, where I made a study of the breeding blackbirds for comparison with the Botanic Garden, the birds themselves were so shy that few details of their behaviour could be seen and I was forced to restrict my enquiry to what could be found out from an examination of the nests.

Garden blackbirds are not difficult to trap. Apart from a few caught at night with nets and occasional birds caught in other ways, all the adults that I ringed were caught in 'Potter traps' (wire traps with a raised door, sliding on runners, which the bird automatically trips as it enters to take the bait). I trapped mainly during the winter, especially in hard weather, in early spring, when young birds were taking up territories, and again in summer, when old and young birds are strongly attracted by cherries and other fruit. I found that it was a waste of time to try to trap in autumn, when fruit is so abundant that the birds are not attracted to the bait, and usually a waste of time to trap during mild weather in winter. Trapping had little or no effect on the birds' subsequent behaviour. An hour or two after being caught they were usually back in their normal routine, and within a day or two they were as fearless of human beings as before. But nearly all the old birds remained trap-shy, and I rarely caught one twice in the same year. Some juveniles, however, kept getting trapped.

I usually ringed the nestlings when they were eight days old. I gave each a numbered ring (issued by the British Trust for Ornithology) and one or more coloured rings. In 1953 I gave members of the same brood the same colour-combination, but from 1954 onwards I gave each nestling in addition an individual colour. This became important later when I found that parents do not feed all their youngsters indiscriminately; it also made it easier to follow the survival of fledglings accurately.

In my records every colour-ringed adult was given a number, prefixed by '♂' or '♀' according to the sex. Juveniles were given a number only after they had moulted into their first-year plumage and so revealed their sex. In the pages that follow I have frequently used these numbers when writing of known birds. This serves to emphasize that they were individuals and not just anonymous blackbirds; in addition it enables the reader to recognize the same individual in different contexts.

This book is in no sense a monograph. I have deliberately concentrated on aspects of the blackbird's life that have interested me. Even on these aspects I have not attempted to cite all the interesting observations that have been made by others, but have referred only to some of those that are particularly apposite, and especially to those that fill in gaps where my own observations were inadequate. On territory, voice and displays, dealt with in Chapters 4–8, there have been some long and detailed papers and the findings of some authors do not agree with my own. To take account of these contributions in the main text would seriously interrupt the story of my own observations. I have therefore discussed them separately in Appendix 2.

The substance of the chapter on territory has already appeared in *The Ibis*, while I have dealt with various aspects of breeding in papers in *Bird Study* and *The Ibis*. But information given in the rest of this book has not appeared in any other form. I have gone into the question of blackbird numbers and given my own data in rather more detail than is, perhaps, consistent with the rest of the book. This is, I think, justified by the inherent interest of the subject, though probably not by my success in solving the problems raised.

In recent years so many books have appeared on single bird species that anyone writing a new one must feel a need to justify it. My excuse is that I am dealing with a bird with which almost everybody is familiar, which is of interest biologically because it is an extremely successful species, and yet has not been adequately dealt with in any book easily available to English readers. A. F. C. Hillstead's *The Blackbird* is unsatisfactory in various ways. *La Vie des Merles*, by Elisabeth Meugens, contains some of the best and most vivid accounts of blackbird behaviour that I have come across, but it is set in semi-fictional form and contains interpretations of behaviour which I believe are wrong in important respects, besides being difficult to obtain. R. Heyder's *Die Amsel* is good, but very brief. The best accounts of special aspects of blackbird behaviour are to be found in ornithological journals.

I am much indebted to the Trustees of the Oxford Botanic Garden for allowing me access to the garden at all times; to the Head Gardener, Mr G. W. Robinson, and his staff for their helpful cooperation; to Timothy Myres and Peter Walters Davies for helping with the field work, especially at times when I was away from Oxford; and to Derek Goodwin for sending me many of his acute observations of blackbird behaviour and illuminating for me some of my own. I have also to thank the Headmaster of Magdalen College School for permission to use the school grounds: in the last two years of the study the half-dozen or so pairs of blackbirds in the school garden were largely colour-ringed and were a useful addition to the Botanic Garden population. I am most grateful to Dr David Lack, Director of the Edward Grey Institute of Field Ornithology, for encouraging these studies, which were a main part of my research during my time at the Institute. Finally, I am indebted to David Lack and R. E. Moreau for valuable and constructive criticism of the manuscript.

—— 2 ——

Plumages and Moults

THE MALE blackbird's plumage, as everybody knows, is completely black. It is a deep sooty black rather than pure jet, and lacks completely the metallic reflexions seen in the plumage of crows and most other black birds. It has a satiny gloss, and in certain lights has a scaly appearance, as the edges of the feathers are less glossy than the inner parts. Females are earth-brown, with pale throats and obscurely spotted breasts. The young are a redder brown than the females, and their looser, fluffier plumage is more spotted below, and above is marked by pale shaft-streaks to the feathers of the mantle and spots on the wing-coverts. In all these plumages there is, however, some variation. To get the most out of watching blackbirds one needs to understand something of these variations and in particular their relation to the moults.

After the sparse down-feathers with which young black-birds are born, the first feathers that grow form the spotted and streaked juvenile plumage. This plumage begins to sprout when the bird is about a week old, and it is worn for about the first three months of its life. When the juvenile plumage is complete, males can usually be distinguished from females. In the males the flight-feathers and tail-feathers are darker, more blackish brown, than in the females: in females they have paler olive-brown edges. The body-plumage also of juvenile males is darker than that of females. In all instances when I have trapped a juvenile, judged its sex on these characters, and later seen the bird after its moult into adult plumage, my diagnosis has been correct. But unfortunately, while the young birds are still in the nest and young enough to be handled without danger of causing them to leave prematurely, the feathers are not advanced enough for these differences to be apparent.

From July onwards juveniles begin to moult into their first adult plumage. This is not quite the same, for reasons which will soon be apparent, as the full adult plumage. I shall call it the first-year plumage, as it is worn through the first year of the bird's adult life, not being changed until the moult of the following autumn. During the moult into first-year plumage, all the feathers are changed except the tail-feathers and some of the wing-feathers. In the wing, the juvenile flight-feathers (except, sometimes, one or two of the inner secondaries), bastard wing, primary coverts, and a variable number of the outer major coverts are retained (Fig. 1). The new feathers that grow are of adult type, but usually duller or paler than those of the full adult plumage. In the male they are not usually so black and the feathers especially of the breast are often edged with brown: in the female the brown is paler

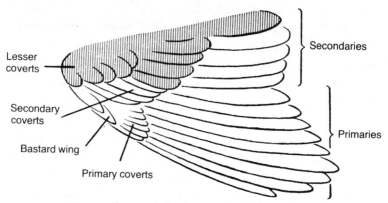

FIG. I. *Wing of typical first-year Blackbird, showing un-moulted juvenile feathers (unshaded) and adult feathers (shaded)*

and more rufous, especially on the breast. Even so, the new feathers contrast with the juvenile wing-feathers and, much less conspicuously, with the juvenile tail. Male blackbirds in first-year plumage can be recognized, often at a considerable distance, by the paler more brownish wings, contrasting with the black of the rest of the plumage. In the field young females can usually be told by their paler, more rufous-coloured under-parts and generally paler upper-parts, but this is not always easy, or even possible, because of the considerable individual variation. If they are close enough, the paler juvenile wing-feathers may be seen, but as the adult wing-feathers are also brown, the distinction is not nearly so clear as in the male. In the hand the two plumages of the female can always be distinguished. The surest way is to examine the row of major coverts: in first-year birds there is a distinct break between the old, juvenile feathers—paler, more rufous, more worn, and with sometimes a trace of the pale terminal spot—and the darker olive-brown adult feathers.

The moult from juvenile to first-year plumage lasts about

five weeks for each bird, beginning with the body-feathers
and wing-coverts and ending with the head. The moult of
the head is completed slowly, so that for the last fortnight of
the moult the general appearance of the bird is of an adult
with a juvenile head, often very ragged and bare. In late
summer these somewhat vulturine young blackbirds are a
familiar sight. The time this moult begins seems to depend
mainly on some external environmental factor, perhaps day-
length, but it also depends partly on the age of the bird,
which may have been born at any time from late March to
July. Most juveniles moult in August or September, whenever they were born: those that were born earliest moult
first, but not so much earlier than the others as they would
if the time of moult depended only on age. I have records of
the interval between leaving the nest and completion of the
moult for twenty-nine colour-ringed birds. For four which
left the nest in April this interval ranged from 117 to 136
days, with an average of 127: for six birds which left the nest
in July the interval ranged from 78 to 90 days, with an average
of 86. For the nineteen which left the nest in May and June
the interval averaged 112 days.

First-year plumages vary considerably, some being rather
close to the adult plumage and some very distinct. Yearling
males, in particular, may be almost as black and glossy as full
adults, or almost as brown as old females, with the whitish
throat of a female. German ornithologists, who have paid
some attention to these variations, have called the first-year
plumage which is close to the full adult plumage 'Fortschritts-
kleid' (advanced plumage) and the other extreme 'Hem-
mungskleid' (retarded plumage).[3] Males in retarded first-
year plumage are known to German bird-catchers as 'Stockamsel'. It has been supposed, though without definite evidence, that birds with advanced first-year plumage are those

that were hatched early in the year and those with retarded plumage are late-hatched birds. The suggested explanation for this is that when the late-hatched birds moult, the development of their gonads is so little advanced that not enough of the hormone controlling the production of male or female plumage is present to exercise its full effect, with the result that a plumage intermediate between adult and juvenile is produced. My own observations do not support this, but I have seen too few first-year birds of known age with retarded plumage for any firm conclusion. The most extreme example that I had of a 'Stockamsel' male, a bird so brown that on a hasty glance it would have been taken for an adult female, left the nest on June 6th, not a very late date. Its brother of the same age moulted into perfectly normal first-year plumage.

Even if this explanation is not true for the difference between advanced and retarded first-year plumage, it nevertheless seems that the increase in sex-hormone in the growing bird progressively affects the colour of the juvenile feathers. Sommerfeld,[69] who made a detailed study of the blackbird's juvenile plumage, pointed out that the juvenile body-feathers do not all develop at the same time. As the young bird grows, the already existing feathers no longer provide a sufficient cover, and new feathers appear along the edges of the main feather-tracts. He compared these new feathers to new pieces of cloth let into children's clothes as they are outgrown. They may be distinguished from the older juvenile feathers by their more adult colouring, in males blacker than the older feathers and in females more olive-coloured, with less extensive shaft-streaks. They are most conspicuous on the back, where they form a backward-pointing V with the two arms overlying the folded wings.

The beak and eye-rim of the juvenile are dark, and stay

dark for some time after the first-year plumage is acquired. The uniformly sooty appearance of first-year males in early autumn must be familiar to all who have watched blackbirds at this season. The change of the beak and eye-rim to yellow in the male normally takes place in the course of the first winter, but the exact time varies a great deal. Some young males show yellow at the base of the beak in September and have fully yellow beaks by the end of November: others still have dark beaks in March. The eye-rim turns yellow at the same time as the beak. The beak and eye-rim of the first-year male, even when they have become completely yellow, are usually not as bright as those of the older males. First-year females do not usually acquire yellow, or even partly yellow, beaks until their first breeding season, and not always then.

The next moult comes when the birds are just over a year old, in their second autumn, and this moult is complete, all the feathers being changed. For each bird it lasts about two months, usually starting in July, when the breeding season is ending. As far as can be seen in the field, it starts simultaneously with the wings, tail and body, and like the first autumn moult ends with the head. After the second-autumn moult the plumage does not change appreciably at succeeding moults, except perhaps in some females, which seem to become a little darker with age. In males, once the beak and eye-rim have become yellow they stay yellow, but become duller in autumn than at other times of year. Females in full adult plumage usually have more or less yellow or yellow-orange beaks in the breeding season, but they become dull and dark again each autumn.

Albino and partially albino blackbirds are more often seen than albinos of any other British bird. I knew of several in Oxford, but was never lucky enough to have one among my colour-ringed population. Different explanations for albinism in blackbirds have been put forward, and indeed the causes may be diverse. There is an early account of a blackbird said to have turned white through fright.[63] More recently it has been suggested that albinism may be caused by a deficient diet, and it is pointed out that albinos are relatively commoner in urban and suburban than in rural habitats.[58] To what extent it is also hereditary is uncertain. There are records of normally coloured parents producing albino offspring, and of albino parents producing normal young; but both would be expected if albinism occurred as a recessive hereditary condition. Whatever its cause, albinism is often progressive, the white areas of the plumage becoming more extensive in successive years.[70] The head and fore part of the body are often the first, and most extensively, affected. Albinism, even if nearly total, does not seem to be an appreciable disadvantage for urban or suburban blackbirds: there are several records of albinos living for years and breeding successfully. But it might be a disadvantage in areas where hawks are commoner.

—————3—————

Food and Feeding Habits

BLACKBIRDS in suburban Oxford eat a great variety of food, most of which falls into five main categories:

Earthworms, mainly from lawns and playing fields, taken all the year round but least in late summer and autumn.

Other concealed food items, mostly immobile or inactive invertebrates, routed out from leaf litter, dug up from the soil, or extracted from rough pasture, and taken all the year round.

Various fruits, indigenous and exotic, taken from July to December, but especially in October and November.

Caterpillars and adult insects living above ground, taken in late spring and summer.

Food put out or thrown out by man, taken especially in hard weather in winter and during summer droughts.

A very simple but well-tried method will show accurately

how a bird's feeding habits change during the year. Several times each month the observer makes a round of a chosen area and notes where each bird was feeding when first seen, making an attempt to get a record for every bird in the area. I used this method to investigate the feeding habits of blackbirds round Oxford. I excluded the Botanic Garden itself, where the mixture of lawns, flower-beds, paths, rough grass

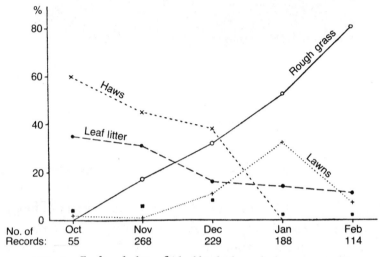

FIG. 2. *Feeding habits of Blackbirds through the autumn and winter in Christ Church Meadow. (Squares: miscellaneous feeding places.)*

and bushes is so complex that birds are continually moving from one to the other and observations are hard to classify, and concentrated instead on surrounding habitats of a simpler nature. Fig. 2 shows the results of observations made in autumn and winter in Christ Church Meadow, a large area of rough grassland and playing fields, with trees and hawthorn hedges along damp ditches. It adjoins the Botanic Garden and many of the garden birds feed there in winter. Haws were the most important single food until December, while at the

26

end of the winter rough grassland provided most of the food. There was little feeding on lawns while the fruit was in season: later, the amount of food taken from lawns depended mainly on the weather. In mild and damp weather worms are easily obtained, and lawns and playing fields are favourite feeding grounds. But in freezing weather, which in the two years in question came mainly in February, this food becomes inaccessible.

By observation it is not easy to determine whether blackbirds find worms by eye or by ear, or whether they use both methods. I believe that they usually find worms by eye, by seeing the tip protruding above the top of the burrow, but that they can also detect and even locate animals moving under the soil by ear. The familiar cocking of the head to one side does not give much of a clue, as this might help the bird either to fix an object with its eye or to determine its position by ear. As evidence for location by ear, in the absence of experiments it is only possible to cite examples of immediate and successful capture of prey that was almost certainly hidden from sight. I have often watched a blackbird, at close quarters, suddenly dig into a lawn and extract a cockchafer larva from well below the surface. Once in a dry oakwood in the Atlas Mountains, in late May, while I sat watching a blue tit's nest, a blackbird approached to within a few feet without seeing me, darted forward, and in an instant extracted a large worm from hard parched earth under a covering of dead leaves. Whatever the method of locating them, blackbirds can pull out worms from lawns with remarkable efficiency: a series of timed counts made in December and January showed that in mild weather they can catch them at the rate of one or two a minute. Often they pull up more than they can eat and leave some of them lying untouched on the surface.

They swallow worms whole when feeding themselves. When taking them to their young they usually chop them into pieces, or simply mangle them without succeeding in breaking them up, by repeatedly beating them against the ground and shaking them. If a dry flower bed is at hand, they often drag the mangled worm through the soil before offering it to the young, perhaps to remove the slime or perhaps because a certain amount of grit is a necessary part of the young bird's diet.

When searching for food among leaf litter or loose earth, blackbirds make use of a coordinated movement of foot and beak. As the beak comes down to flick, or momentarily seize and throw to one side, the dead leaves or earth, one foot comes forward to the level of the head and scratches vigorously backwards. This combined movement is very effective in laying bare otherwise inaccessible food, and in winter it enables blackbirds to dig down through as much as two or three inches of snow. It also enables them to exploit some unlikely feeding niches. A favourite one in Oxford is the line of moss that grows on narrow ledges on the outside of old stone buildings. In winter blackbirds work along these lines of moss, showering pieces on to the ground below, and finish by scraping them away completely. They also habitually rummage among leaf litter and other debris that has collected in thick creepers or among the bunches of twigs growing from tree trunks.

Caterpillars and adult insects are taken mainly when young are being fed. Indeed, as will be discussed later, I believe that the timing of the breeding season is adapted, in part, to the seasonal abundance of this food. In deciduous woodland near Oxford, a habitat which is certainly closer to the blackbird's ancestral habitat than suburban garden and parkland, I found that caterpillars were the chief food of the young for most of the breeding season. In the Botanic Garden the situation was different. Earthworms, in which the area is so rich, were nearly always the chief food of the young. Adult insects increased in importance in the young birds' diet as the breeding season advanced, but caterpillars were important for only one limited period during the course of my study, in late May 1956, when a severe drought made worms unavailable. At this time caterpillars were falling in large numbers from a line of trees just outside the garden and blackbirds were coming from as far as two and three hundred yards away to collect them.

From about mid-May onwards, the skin of nearly all the nestlings that I examined in woodland was tinged with yellow, sometimes very conspicuously. I never noticed it in nestlings examined in late April, before caterpillars are numerous, and only once in nestlings in early May. Nor did I ever notice it in any of the Botanic Garden nestlings, whose skin was the usual dull pink. It seems most likely that the pigment is derived from the green caterpillars on which the woodland nestlings are so largely fed in late May and June. Derek Goodwin has found the same yellow deposit in the skin of nestling jays, which are also fed on green caterpillars. He tells me that it does not occur in captive young jays reared on ant pupae, meal worms, etc., but it does in captive young fed on caterpillars.

Fruit forms, at least in bulk, the blackbird's chief food from late summer to early winter. As is well known, almost any soft fruit is taken. In August and September various exotic trees come into fruit in the Botanic Garden, but a large mulberry tree in Merton College garden, about 200 yards away, is even more favoured and attracts birds from the whole neighbourhood. In October and November, large numbers of blackbirds collect to feed on two large Sorbus trees in the

Botanic Garden, while later, in December, the hawthorns just outside the garden attract even larger numbers.

The tendency to peck at red and shiny objects seems to be innate. A captive young blackbird, which almost certainly could not have eaten cherries before, since the cherry season had not started when it was caught, pecked at them at once when they were offered. It preferred red ones to yellow, as do blackbirds in the wild, and was also attracted to other shiny objects such as polished shoes.

When all other food fails, blackbirds turn to that provided by man. During summer droughts they are sometimes reduced to feeding their young on bread: at such times I have often watched a parent bird, undeterred by the unsuitability of the food, trying repeatedly to make its offspring swallow a dry crust. But it is during very hard weather in winter that food provided directly by man becomes important. The Botanic Garden blackbirds then spend much of their time away from their territories, visiting back gardens for scraps. On such a diet, supplemented by the little natural food that they can find, they can survive for many days. In three of the four winters during which I was watching the Botanic Garden birds there were unusually cold spells, two of them prolonged. Nevertheless only one-eighth of my population disappeared during these periods, and some of their deaths may well have been due to tawny owls and other causes unconnected with starvation.

The older bird books usually list snails among the blackbird's food. Blackbirds certainly eat small snails, which they swallow whole, and they also rob song thrushes of the larger snails when the latter have extracted them from their shells; but it seems that blackbirds have not the ability to break open snail shells for themselves. Morris,[52] who made a detailed study of the snail-eating behaviour of song thrushes, showed that the successful breaking open of a shell involves the selection of a suitable 'anvil', the gripping of the shell by the rim of the aperture, and a special action of the head and neck by which the snail is rhythmically hammered against the anvil with sufficient force to break the shell—coordinated behaviour which is not in the blackbird's repertory. If blackbirds could open snail shells in this way it would certainly be an advantage for them, for song thrushes turn to snails at times when other food is short, and in droughts, for example, are able to feed their young largely on snails when young blackbirds are starving in the nests.

Blackbirds habitually rob smaller birds of their food. Everybody who has watched birds in a garden will have noticed how often, as soon as a house sparrow, chaffinch or song thrush has found a morsel, a blackbird rushes up and drives the smaller bird away. In most cases the blackbird reacts to the sight of another bird holding the food in its beak or extracting something from the ground; but in the case of song thrushes with snails Morris found that, if the thrush is out of sight, the blackbird reacts to the cessation of the sound of hammering, the sign that the snail is in a state in which it can be dealt with by the blackbird.

When mixed flocks of thrushes are feeding in winter on open playing fields, food-robbing goes on continually. Blackbirds rob redwings and song thrushes, and are themselves robbed, though less often, by mistle thrushes and fieldfares. As well as being more persistent robbers than the two larger birds, the blackbirds show a more extreme development of the behaviour. While mistle thrushes and fieldfares will drive a smaller bird away from food if it is within a few feet, blackbirds will rush up, half running and half flying, from several yards away to attack another bird, beginning their attack as soon as they see their victim pulling a worm out of the ground.

The only smaller species which the blackbird cannot normally rob of food is the starling. Starlings, profiting by their sharp, strong beaks, not infrequently threaten blackbirds and force them to give up their food, whereas blackbirds hardly ever succeed in robbing starlings. I saw only three individual blackbirds in the Botanic Garden, each on only one occasion, succeed in robbing starlings, and two of these birds were known to be unusually aggressive. Young blackbirds apparently learn by experience that they must submit to starlings. Old birds do not usually attempt to rob them, but juveniles often try and I have several times seen first-year birds trying to do so during hard weather in winter. The starling, when threatened, is not perturbed, but without yielding ground simply turns and repels the blackbird with a jab of the beak.

It can hardly be coincidence that in flight chases between blackbirds and other species, which are especially frequent in autumn, the dominance relations which hold good on the ground are exactly reversed. In the air, blackbirds chase mistle thrushes and starlings and are regularly chased by song thrushes, chaffinches and house sparrows. The reversal of dominance between the blackbird and song thrush is particularly striking, as encounters between them are so common. Only twice have I seen a blackbird chase a song thrush in flight: one was a very perfunctory chase, soon broken off, and the other involved a juvenile blackbird. On the other hand, song thrushes often chase blackbirds in the air over long distances. Hardly less striking is the tendency for chaffinches to chase blackbirds in flight. The reaction seems almost automatic. Several times, when I have been watching a blackbird in flight, it has passed close to a chaffinch on the ground and the chaffinch has instantly set off in pursuit. These flight chases seem entirely functionless. So regular is the reversal of dominance that it is difficult to avoid the anthropomorphic suggestion that the bird which is worsted in the more serious encounters on the ground harbours a grudge against the aggressor which finds relief in a form of attack that is little more than a gesture. The motivation may be fundamentally the same as that which leads to the mobbing of predators.

At this point there will be no need to stress again the versatility of blackbirds. In addition to the main types of food and feeding method discussed above, some more remarkable ones can be mentioned. Blackbirds have been seen catching slow-worms, taking tadpoles and small fish out of streams, and catching insects in the air. Sometimes they wash their food before eating it. No doubt in other parts of their range other sources of food than those discussed may be of regular importance. This versatility and adaptability appears early in life: juvenile blackbirds spend much of their time, when they are becoming independent of their parents, testing all sorts of objects, edible and inedible. The behaviour of these young birds, as they jump up and peck at flowers, or gingerly prod bumble bees, though amusing to watch, with its suggestion of play, is the expression of innate tendencies that are of real importance to the species. There is little doubt that the ability of blackbirds to exploit a wide variety of food sources, and to switch quickly from one to the other, is one of the chief factors enabling them to maintain a dense population in a richly diverse area such as the Oxford Botanic Garden.

---4---

The Territory

GARDEN BLACKBIRDS are strongly territorial, and it is against the background of their attachment to a particular piece of land that most of the activities of their life should be viewed. The territory is normally a compact area whose borders can be mapped with some accuracy, though they may swiftly alter. In the Botanic Garden the average size of a territory was about half an acre. The acquiring of a territory is one of the main events in the life of a young male during his first year, while the holding of it occupies old males intermittently throughout their lives. The territorial behaviour of females is more variable. They are normally less territorial than males, simply accepting the territories owned by their mates, but some females may be as strong as their mates in the defence of their territories and a few hold territories of their own for limited periods. Mated pairs usually stay together in the territory all the year round.

The strength of the territorial urge varies at different seasons, being at its strongest just before breeding begins. But it is most convenient to begin the description of the annual territorial cycle with the moult, when territorial behaviour is at its weakest, for this forms the real break between one blackbird's year and the next. The moult follows the end of the breeding season. While moulting the adults keep mainly to their old territories, making occasional excursions to neighbouring fruit trees. Juveniles, which at the same time are moulting to first-year plumage, are sometimes perfunctorily attacked but mainly tolerated. Few aggressive encounters are seen. As early as the end of August, but more usually in September, territorial borders begin to be defined again. By October the boundaries can again be mapped, on the basis of border disputes, and are largely the same as in the previous breeding season. Throughout the autumn the old territory-owners continue to visit fruit trees, some birds spending considerable parts of the day away from their territories. I have often seen ringed birds up to about a quarter of a mile away from their territories, but not much further. They do not usually trespass in territories adjoining their own.

From a very early age juveniles show a preference for particular areas. Young birds, recently independent of their parents, resort day after day to favourite feeding places, perhaps a certain group of flower-beds, or the moist corner of a field. By September the tendency to settle is even more marked. Nevertheless at this early stage these preferred areas are by no means continuously occupied, and they are often abandoned, possibly because of changes in the availability of food.

Juvenile males vary considerably in the time that they take

to establish themselves permanently, depending, it seems, largely on whether their early preference is for a place which is suitable and, later, available as a future territory. Each year I had one or two young males which from autumn onwards frequented a chosen part of the garden, and they gradually, with little or no opposition from other males, established themselves by the end of the winter, even though they were not continuously present. More often young males temporarily annex part of an old bird's territory, defending it for a time against the former owner and the neighbours. In most of the instances which I have seen, these small annexed territories, which are most characteristic of autumn and early winter, have been given up as suddenly as they were occupied, as a result of continuing opposition from the established owners or of changes in the local food supply; the bird then reverts to an unsettled existence, and it is not until February or March that the definitive breeding territory is occupied. It appears as if the 'drive' to take up a territory becomes active in young males in autumn, but is not at full strength until the end of the winter. Territorial behaviour in the early stages also has a marked diurnal rhythm. It is mainly in the early morning that the young males are to be seen in their incipient territories: later in the day the same birds may be found feeding communally in fields and along hedges a few hundred yards away.

Juvenile females show the same tendency to resort to favoured areas, which they defend against other females and sometimes against males, but many of them form apparent pairs with the owning males, whether they be old widowed males (five cases observed), old paired males whose mates are temporarily absent (four cases), or young males (five cases). As will be seen later, these apparent pairs break up before the breeding season begins. A few young females hold

territories of their own for limited periods in areas where
there happens to be no resident male.

An unusually large number of autumn territories were
established by young birds in 1955, and their maintenance
was related to the presence of locally abundant fruit. From
as early as August ♀52, a bird born in the garden at the end
of April, showed a consistent preference for one corner of
the garden, though she was also seen feeding elsewhere, and
by the end of September she had a small territory from which
she vigorously excluded other young birds. This was entirely
within the territory of an old pair, but at first she was never
seen in conflict with them, probably because they were still
moulting and their territorial behaviour was quiescent. On
October 9th ♀52 was engaged in aggressive display with a
young male, ♂61, who had been born near by but had not
been seen since June, and later in the day she had a violent
fight with him. She was evidently worsted as she soon after
abandoned her territory and ♂61 took it over. On October
16th another young female, ♀65, was holding a small territory next to that of ♂61, and was seen in aggressive display
with him on the border. But she was dominated by the old
resident male and, perhaps because of this, did not remain
for more than a week. ♂61 meanwhile maintained and expan-
ded his territory, and fought with the old female, effectively
excluding her from his territory. The old male was spending
almost all his time in another part of the territory and was
not seen in conflict with ♂61 until November 13th, when he
too was excluded from the ground which ♂61 held.

During the whole of October and the first half of November there was an unusually abundant crop of fruit in the
garden, especially from two Sorbus trees near where these
small territories had been established, and many young birds,
and trespassing old birds, were visiting the garden. By early

November two other young males had small territories near the fruit trees. The fruit supply came to an end rather suddenly between November 17th and 20th, the fallen remnants being swept up by the gardeners, and at the same time the young birds nearly all disappeared, including ♂61 and one of the other males which had a territory. The other young male with a territory abandoned it at the end of the month. None of the ringed birds involved, ♂61, ♀52 and ♀65, was later seen to try to establish itself in this area. Even while their occupation of the territories was at its height, they spent only part of the day in them, being usually absent in the afternoons. The territories were all very small (except for that of ♂61 in its later stages), measuring not more than 10 to 20 yards across.

On mild days in autumn, when a number of young birds are feeding together on hawthorns and other fruit trees, the aggressive tendencies which, especially in the early morning, lead to the incipient territorial behaviour described above, find expression in wild flight-chases in and out of the trees and bushes. Old birds have never been seen taking part in these chases. The pursuing bird is most often a young male, the pursued bird a young male or female.

The general situation described above, with the old pairs retaining their territories and a few young birds establishing themselves, usually temporarily, in small territories, persists through most of the winter, as long as the weather is mild, with a steady increase in aggressive behaviour by old birds which leads to greater definition of territory boundaries. Spells of cold weather interrupt the process, and if severe enough may cause a total break-down of territories, at least during the greater part of the day—roosting sites, which are mainly within the territories, appear to remain unchanged. Birds then wander in search of food, most leaving their territories and resorting to sheltered spots beneath trees and bushes, where the abundant leaf litter remains unfrozen, or to food put out by man in adjacent gardens, while those that remain in their territories are more tolerant of intruders. In the cold spell of early 1954 and that of early 1955, males left their territories much more than females. In both 1954 and 1955 the cold spells came to an end in February and the territorial behaviour which had been arrested for two or three weeks quickly reached a climax, while in 1953, with no late cold spell, it mounted more gradually from January onwards.

In the month or so before breeding begins, old males become completely intolerant of other male blackbirds; most of the young males succeed in establishing themselves, by taking over vacant areas or by inserting themselves at the junctions and interstices between already occupied territories, and the definitive territories for the start of the breeding season are formed. Meanwhile the old surviving pairs persist, either having remained together all winter, or, as happened in two cases, re-forming on the return of the female who has spent most of the winter elsewhere (in the immediate neighbourhood, in both cases). There was only one case, among my colour-ringed birds, of a pair which survived the winter parting company and taking new mates in the following breeding season. On the other hand, most of the apparent pairs formed during the winter prove not to be true pairs, the females moving elsewhere, usually not far, and pairing with other males. More new pairs are formed at this time (late February and early March) than at any other.

The stage is thus set for nesting, but the pairs and territories so formed do not remain fixed right through to the end of the breeding season. There are several ways in which changes may occur. One of a pair may die. If the female dies, the male stays in his territory and usually sings persistently.

This has been so in the seven cases that I observed, in only two of which the male obtained a new mate, while in the other five he remained unmated until the end of the season. If the male dies the female either moves away (five cases), or she may remain in the territory (three cases). In six of these eight cases the female was known to have mated again later in the season, while in the other two she was not seen again. Sometimes a pair shifts together, usually but not always after failure to breed successfully. Arrivals and departures of these shifting pairs may cause extensive alteration of territories, by contraction due to the establishment of newcomers or by expansion into vacated areas. In addition, minor alterations in boundaries may occur at any time. They are often caused by the female choosing a nest-site on or even beyond the territory border, in which case the male actively extends the territory in that direction.

The vigour with which territorial boundaries are defined declines throughout the breeding season, but not steadily. Each pair shows a well-marked rhythm of territorial activity corresponding with each attempt to nest. Defence is strongest when the female is choosing a nest-site and building, becomes weakest when the young are in the nest, and stronger again when the next nest is started. This rhythm is so marked that late in the season it is usually safe to assume that if a male is seen engaging his neighbours in conflict his mate is starting or about to start a new nest. When neighbouring pairs have their nests, and hence their territorial rhythms, out of step, there may be rapid alterations in boundaries which appear confusing if the nesting history of each pair is not known. This was particularly well shown by three pairs in 1954. The first brood of pair A ($\male$9, $\female$24) left the nest successfully on April 25th. On May 9th, while they were still being fed near the nest, the male of pair B ($\male$11, $\female$22) was found to be persistently intruding and had soon driven a deep wedge into pair A's territory, while his mate was building a nest only six yards from pair A's old nest. Two days earlier, pair C (♂24, ♀20, both young birds and only recently paired) had also started, less obtrusively, to build a nest only about ten yards from pair A's old nest. The first eggs were laid in these two new nests within two days of one another, and both nests were successful. When both had young, and the territorial behaviour of the parents was consequently weak, pair A in their turn, now ready to start their second nest, succeeded in reclaiming the greater part of their territory, and the female renewed her old nest and had laid the first egg in it before the young had flown from the nests of pairs B and C. Thus three nests, all within ten yards of one another, were occupied at the same time.

By the end of the breeding season, when most pairs are feeding their last families of young, and few or none are beginning new nests, territorial behaviour is weak. Even those adults that have been most sedentary in previous weeks are now regularly to be seen trespassing with impunity in their neighbours' territories, often accompanied by their young, who do not remain so long near the nest as do the young from earlier broods. This situation passes gradually into the almost complete cessation of territorial activity that accompanies the moult.

The shapes and distribution of territories from year to year were rather stable in the Botanic Garden (Fig. 3). This stability was due largely to the fact that adults usually retain their territories as long as they live, and two-thirds of them survived from one year to the next; but it was also partly due to the distribution of cover. Some clumps of cover form natural headquarters for territories, while areas where the cover is sparse are not defended so strongly. This was very

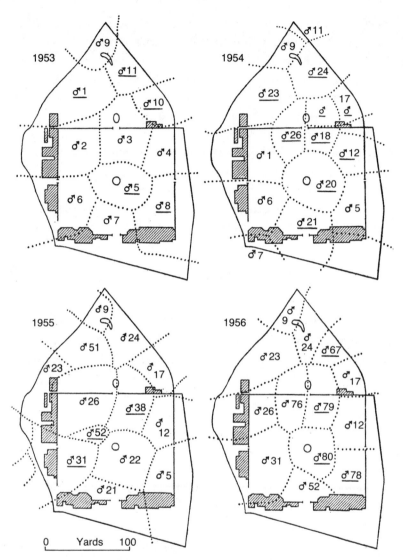

FIG. 3. *Blackbird territories in the Oxford Botanic Garden in four years; shown as they were in late March, at the beginning of the breeding season. Underlined figures indicate young males born the previous season.*

well illustrated in the walled part of the garden. The central area is rather open and contains trees, lawns and flower-beds, but hardly any suitable cover for a nest, while the creeper-covered walls all round have an abundance of good nest-sites. In each of the four years the central area was claimed by a young male—always of course a different one—and in each year its territory was more or less the same shape and size, as the neighbours were in part the same birds in successive years and yielded ground to about the same limits. Each year the young male obtained a mate and the pair tried to breed in their territory, but failed, because of predation or desertion of their too exposed nests. They then succeeded in extending their territory to one of the walls, where all their later nests were built. The piece of creeper-covered wall which they annexed was the same in each year, apparently because the territories on either side remained more or less the same size and shape and the females in them always chose nest-sites in more central parts of their territories: this particular stretch of wall was in consequence weakly defended.

In gardens and park-like habitats round Oxford it is usual to see young males, in February and March, singing, sometimes for several days in succession, high up in trees. In 1954 three such birds habitually sang from high trees in the Botanic Garden, unable to establish themselves on the ground below which was already occupied. One at least of these birds later established itself when a territory fell vacant. In more open parkland, young males may sing from quite isolated trees in the middle of open ground, where they could not possibly nest, but I have not found these birds remaining long in such places. Thus it seems that whereas a suitable nest-site is ultimately the most important element in a territory, a suitable song-post is all that is initially necessary to attract a young male in search of a territory.

It may be the young male's interest in nest-sites that ensures that he eventually chooses a suitable territory. We shall see later that males, and especially young males, prospect for nest-sites as well as females, but do not actually build. Usually they prospect in company with their mates, but not always, and once I saw a young male prospecting before he had acquired a mate. There is little doubt that the actual site used is usually chosen by the female, but the interest shown by the male is probably of real value in ensuring that his mate has suitable nest-sites available to her.

Territories are defended by males mainly against males, and by females mainly against females. The males are usually more active than their mates in the maintenance of territory. But there is much individual variability. Some males frequently drive out females, and some females males, and individual females may be much more active than their mates. Most disputes are settled by display, which will be described in a later chapter: territorial fighting, in which the contestants actually come to blows, is common only at times when young males are carving out territories for themselves, when males are extending their territories, and, to a lesser extent, during the resurgence of territorial activity when a pair is starting a second or third nest. Such fights are usually short-lived: occasionally, as we shall see in a later chapter, they may be bitter and lead to death.

Established adults do not drive out all intruders indiscriminately. It is clear that they recognize individually all their established neighbours, and also many of the local unestablished young birds. This is strikingly seen when several birds have gathered to feed on fallen fruit within an old bird's territory. The owner will often single out and drive off one of its neighbours, disregarding other trespassers, or will pay particular attention to an individual young bird that is trying to take up a territory next to or partly within its own, disregarding other young birds which may be feeding much closer to it. It is clear that territorial defence is directed particularly against individuals that represent a potential threat to the owner's territory.

It appears essential for a male to have a territory in order to obtain a mate. Often, in early spring, both are acquired almost simultaneously, especially when a male obtains possession of a territory on or near which an unmated female is settled. In other cases it may be some weeks before the male obtains a mate. I knew of only one young male, ♂19, that failed to obtain a territory during what should have been his first breeding season. From March to July he frequented a number of different areas, already occupied by established pairs, in and a short distance outside the Botanic Garden. He never had a mate.

Once a male has obtained a mate, defence of the territory is to some extent modified so as to include defence of the female. This is most noticeable when the female is building. At this time he will constantly accompany her, first when she is prospecting for nest-sites and later when she is collecting nest-material. He is especially aggressive to other males at this time, and will even behave aggressively towards a male in whose territory he has trespassed in company with his mate. It is this solicitous defence of the female which leads him to enlarge the boundaries of the territory if she chooses a nest-site near the border.

Blackbirds are by no means dependent on their territories for their food, though they get a good deal of it there. Actually, territories break down most completely when food is scarcest. As already mentioned, during cold spells in winter most birds move away from their territories and seek food elsewhere, and those that stay are more tolerant of intruders.

In autumn and early winter, when food is locally abundant outside their territories, birds also frequently leave their territories and spend large parts of the day on hawthorns and other berry-bearing trees. The owners of the territories containing these fruit trees show perfunctory hostility to the intruders but make no sustained attempt to drive them away.

All the territories in the Botanic Garden have contained an area of lawn and flower-bed. For the early broods much of the food is found within the territory, because earthworms, their chief diet, are easily obtained early in the season when territorial behaviour is at its strongest. But for later broods most of the food is obtained outside the garden, particularly from the low-lying playing field of Magdalen College School near by, which still affords worms when the lawns and flower-beds have dried up. In dry weather in June, twenty or thirty blackbirds may be seen collecting worms on this field, for nests in the Botanic Garden and neighbouring gardens. Thus neither in winter nor in the breeding season does the territory guarantee the owners an adequate supply of food.

The function of territory in birds has been much debated in the last thirty years. There has been no general agreement, but at least it is now clear that territories are of many types, that they do not all have the same function, and that it is no longer useful to speak broadly of 'the function of territory': each species or group of species must be considered separately. What then is the value to the blackbird of its strong and continuous urge to defend a territory?

As we have seen, the intensity of territorial behaviour through the year fluctuates with reproductive activities, which suggests that its chief function must be sought in relation to breeding. Territorial behaviour increases in intensity as the breeding season approaches, culminates at the time when building begins, and is at its lowest just after breeding has finished. In addition, it waxes and wanes with each nesting cycle. Eliot Howard, who brought into prominence the subject of territory in birds, suggested that one function of a breeding territory was to conserve an adequate food supply for the young. This suggestion appeared to lose some of its force when it was found that many territorial birds obtain only a part of the food for the young, or sometimes none of it, within the territory. The blackbird is one of these. Nevertheless it must be borne in mind that if the territorial behaviour has initially spaced out the breeding pairs to the right extent, it could in this way ensure a sufficient amount of food for each pair and their young, whether or not the birds later forage beyond the borders of their territories. But neither for blackbirds nor for any other birds have we the measurements of territory-size, abundance of food, and amount of food required by each family, that would enable us to test this suggestion.

It has also been suggested that the spacing out of the breeding pairs, which is one of the results of territorial behaviour, reduces the chance that the nests will be found by predatory animals.[75] Finding one nest will be no indication to a predator that others may be found near by: predators will thus develop no special bias towards this particular prey, as they are known to do towards prey that is available in quantity. Blackbirds' nests are open to destruction by a large number of different predators, and anything promoting their safety will have a strong selective advantage. It is certainly no coincidence that colonially nesting birds are in general those that can effectively defend their nests—among thrushes, for example, the fieldfare—or those that breed in inaccessible places or in places where predators are rare.

The extension of the blackbird's territorial behaviour from the breeding season to the greater part of the year needs no special explanation. Clearly it is an advantage for old birds to retain the territories where they have already bred, which they know intimately, and where they are psychologically dominant, while for young birds I had direct evidence that it is an advantage to secure a territory as soon as possible. Each year in the Botanic Garden, those young males that were late in acquiring territories paired later and started to breed later than their fellows. At all times of the year, it must be an advantage to a bird to live in an area where it is familiar with all the resources, rather than in a succession of strange places. Natural selection is thus bound, other things being equal, to favour an early and continuous occupation of territory.

It is not very satisfactory to have to suggest two or three explanations for a phenomenon, none of which seems quite sufficient by itself. Yet if we think in terms of the birds' behaviour rather than in the abstractions of the previous paragraphs, the difficulties become less. Territory, and with it each of the suggested advantages conferred by the possession of a territory, depends ultimately on attachment to a fixed area and on aggressiveness towards members of the same species, and especially of the same sex. Attachment to a fixed area is of course essential for a bird, at least during the breeding season. The ability of the bird and its neighbours to learn ensures that each area has more or less fixed boundaries, and so produces that abstraction, 'the territory', which seems to exist as something in its own right.

To sum up, isolation and dispersion of the breeding pairs is an advantage to the blackbird, probably because predation is thereby reduced, and possibly also because if nests were crowded together the food supply for the young would be jeopardized. The necessary degree of isolation between breeding pairs has been brought about by the evolution of strong aggressive tendencies towards members of the same species, and more particularly members of the same sex. The territorial system that has resulted has now, in those populations that do not need to migrate, acquired value at other times of the year also. It ensures that each individual has a piece of ground which it can learn thoroughly, and in which, by knowing all the resources of cover, food and vantage points, it is less liable to predation and other hazards than it would be if it moved about at random over a wider area.

---5---

Song and Calls

THE BLACKBIRD'S mellow warbling song, with its occasional harsh chuckles, is too well known to need to be described. Well known, too, is the fact that the songs of different individuals may differ markedly, and that some have a habit of interpolating imitations of other birds. There is also a striking difference between the dawn song, which is typically staccato, with short, incisive and rather monotonous phrases, and the song given later in the day, which is mellower and more desultory, with longer and more intricate phrasing. Over a hundred years ago Macgillivray (1837) described this well: 'The first morning song of the blackbird is very singular, and altogether different from the evening song, consisting of repetitions of the same unmusical strain, performed with a harsh screaming voice.' There is a seasonal change too: as spring advances the song improves in mellowness and intricacy, just as it does in the course of the day.

In Oxford gardens and parks, full song (to distinguish it from subsong, which will be mentioned later) begins in late winter or very early spring, depending on the weather. In 1953 the first song was heard in the Botanic Garden on February 17th and thereafter it was regular. In 1954 a great outburst of song began on February 12th, when mild, damp weather suddenly succeeded a cold spell, and from then on it continued without a break. In 1955 song was heard on February 4th and 6th, in mild weather, but there was then a cold spell, with snow, until the end of the month and the next song was not heard until March 1st. In 1956 cold weather continued until late into February and the first song did not begin until the 27th. The first song of the year is nearly always heard in the late afternoon, often at dusk; dawn song begins a few days later. Gradually the afternoon song period extends back into the earlier part of the day, so that after two or three weeks song may be heard at any time. But a well-marked diurnal rhythm remains: first a great outburst of song at dawn, lasting twenty minutes to half an hour, then a sudden falling off, followed by a gradual rise throughout the day to the second peak at dusk.

For the first six weeks of the song period, until about the end of March, nearly all day-time song is from young males. Old males sing sporadically at dawn, and on fine evenings at dusk, but hardly at all in the middle of the day. I noticed this early in 1953, and thereafter systematically noted the age of males singing in the early part of the season. From February to mid-March I was able to distinguish the age of 62 singing males, of which all but seven (89 per cent) were first-year birds. In the second half of March I recorded the age of 95 singing males, of which 68 (72 per cent) were first-year birds. The preponderance of the young males' contribution is even more marked than these figures indicate, as most of the earliest records for old birds were of short bursts of song at dusk, whereas young males' song was more sustained as well as being heard at all times of the day.

Most of the old males whose nesting histories were known started regular song at about the same time as their mates laid their first clutches of eggs. Thus at the end of March and beginning of April, when most of the old birds began to nest, there was a conspicuous increase in song in the Botanic Garden. Thereafter the contribution of old and young males seemed to be more nearly equal. Young males probably sang a little more, as some of them continued their early sustained song until well after they had started to breed, while a few old males hardly sang at all; there is great individual variation. Song finishes in July, when breeding ends and the moult begins, and except for the occasional autumn song, which will be mentioned later, is not heard again until the end of the following winter.

Throughout the song period, but especially in the early part, the volume of song depends much on the weather. Mild, still, damp afternoons are most favourable for song in February and March, and the first song is normally heard on such days. Later, though some song may be heard on almost any day, wet, still weather is much more favourable than dry and windy weather; a great outburst of song follows sudden rain at the end of a drought. The end of the song period seems to be hastened by dry weather and prolonged by wet weather: for instance, the last song was recorded on July 8th in the dry summer of 1955, and on July 21st in the wet summer of 1956.

The output of song by individual males varies also according to the stage of the nesting cycle. The amount of song increases while the female is incubating the eggs, then decreases at the time of hatching. Thereafter song remains steady, at a low level. Often, the male sings a snatch of song as he approaches the nest with food in his beak, but he has little time for sustained song. After the young have left the nest, the male continues to feed them for another three weeks, while the female after a few days usually begins a new nest. As they become independent, the male spends more and more of his time singing; by this time the female is usually incubating her next clutch of eggs.

Some ornithologists have suggested that the blackbird's song is functionless. Certainly its function is more puzzling than in many other birds, which sing to advertize ownership of a territory or to attract a mate. Partly this is due to the sporadic nature of blackbird song and to the fact that there are striking differences in the output of song by individual males; partly perhaps to its desultory delivery, which hardly suggests that it is performing any vital function. However, examination of the circumstances in which blackbirds sing provides some clues to its function.

The early spring song of young males is closely connected with their taking up of territories. It is undoubtedly because old males are usually already settled in territories at this time that they are comparatively silent. They are not always silent. In 1955, for instance, an old male whose previous history was unknown suddenly appeared in the Botanic Garden in the first day or two of April and sang persistently in a small area where three territories met. No other old males were singing regularly at this time. After a few days he had enlarged it and established his ownership, and shortly afterwards he obtained a mate and bred.

For some young males, song is important in their search for a territory. These birds, when they have found a suitable area, choose a conspicuous song-post and start to sing. Often this at once attracts the attention of the owning male, and the young bird is quickly driven away. This may be repeated many times, until he eventually finds a place where he can sing undisturbed. Here, after a few days, he becomes psychologically dominant and if the area is suitable the breeding territory may be established. Once ownership is confirmed, song is not noticeably reduced; probably continued assertion of ownership is necessary in order to deter possible competitors.

Other young males sing little until they have secured a firm foothold. During the initial period of searching they remain silent or give only occasional subdued song. In the case of one such bird I was able to see very clearly the connection between ownership of a territory and song. ♂31, a first-year male, had been trying to establish himself since the beginning of February 1955 in a part of the garden which was already fully occupied by old males. He was not heard to sing at all. On March 13th the owner of one of the territories, ♂6, was accidentally poisoned, and by the morning of the 14th he was dead. At half past six that morning, ♂31 was engaged in conflict with another young male, involving fights and extreme aggressive posturing. ♂31 was the more aggressive and evidently had the better of it, as the other male disappeared after about half an hour. A little later, ♂31 was seen courting ♀26, ♂6's mate, and immediately afterwards he sang loudly from a wall in the middle of what had been ♂6's territory. Later that day and the next he was still singing steadily from the same place and his occupation of the territory was not contested.

Though it is thus a signal of prospective or actual ownership of a territory, and to that extent aggressive in import, song is not an aggressive 'weapon' as it is, for instance, in the robin. Males do not engage in song duels: the song of an intruding male who is in search of a territory evokes hostile behaviour from the established owner, but he does not sing back. If an intruding male perches near a territory-owner who is singing, as happens not infrequently, the latter stops singing and advances aggressively towards the intruder. I could see no evidence that song itself causes an intruding bird to retreat, though it may be that males in search of territories tend to avoid places where males are already singing.

The relation of song to the female is not obvious. In early spring, when song is primarily connected with the taking up of territories, males do not noticeably diminish the volume of their song when they obtain a mate. The song of a male is not therefore a good guide for a female in search of a mate. As will be mentioned later, visual displays, sometimes accompanied by a form of subsong, play the chief part in pair-formation. Nevertheless the presence of the mate to some extent inhibits song, probably by diverting the male to other activities, such as the accompanying and guarding of the female and activities connected with the nest. It is probably for this reason that males who have lost their mates sing much more than mated males, and the increase in song when the female is incubating may have the same cause.

Much of the later song, in May and June, does indeed seem functionless. Not only is it desultory, dependent on the weather, and individually variable in amount, but it continues after the other manifestations of territorial activity are noticeably reduced; and some of my old males, who had hardly sung at all earlier in the season when competition for territories was intense, have come into regular song late in the season. Nevertheless song probably serves as a signal of continuing ownership of a territory, and so may be a useful activity when the bird is otherwise at leisure—and the males have more leisure in the latter part of the breeding season. Its individual variation could be explained on the hypothesis that in the blackbird, visual displays can rather easily take over the functions of song. This may be especially so in dense populations like that of the Oxford Botanic Garden, where neighbours are frequently in sight of one another.

On fine days in October and November, short bursts of typical song may occasionally be heard. The singers that I have identified have mainly been young males. This song is loud, typically phrased, and delivered from a high perch, and seems to represent a premature development of the territorial song which properly begins in February. On one occasion, on October 5th, I was watching a young male singing high in a tree when another young male flew into the tree and perched near him. The singing bird at once stopped singing and drove the other away. As has been mentioned earlier, at this time some young males take up territories, usually only for a short time, and there are other signs of incipient territorial and sexual behaviour.

From late September to November, young males are often heard giving a subdued song, rather hurried and jumbled, and interspersed with soft alarm rattles. It may be delivered with the beak closed or only slightly open, from a variety of perches, low and high. Such song seems to have little territorial or aggressive significance: twice only have I seen it directly associated with aggressive behaviour. On one occasion a young male, after singing thus for several minutes perched about a yard from another young male, eventually attacked the other and drove it away. On another occasion a young male, after singing subdued song from a high, exposed perch, was attacked and chased away by a female who had temporarily made herself dominant in the area. But when I have known something of the history of the singing bird, I have never had any evidence that it was trying to establish a territory in the place where it was singing. Rather it appears that such song is given by moderately aggressive birds in fine weather, usually near a place where they have been feeding.

Subdued song seems to be intermediate between full autumn song and subsong. The latter differs chiefly in being much quieter, only audible a few yards away, and delivered with the beak closed and throat barely moving. I have recorded subsong from both old and young males from August right through the winter, but most often from young birds on fine days in October and November. It seems to have no function with respect to other birds, and, as Gurr[21] says, to be given 'for the sole benefit of the performer'. Not only is it audible for only a short distance, but it has a certain ventriloquial quality and is frequently given from thick cover, so that the singer, though only a few feet away, is often very difficult to locate. Birds also give subsong while foraging among leaf litter on the ground, only interrupting it when they suddenly dig for a morsel of food.

A modified form of subsong is sometimes given during display. Often when courting, and less often when engaged in intense threat display with an equally matched rival, males utter a subdued version of the song, hurried and confused and strongly giving the impression that the bird is prevented from singing normally by being strangled. I shall refer to this later as 'strangled song'.

Normally only males sing, but ♀45, an abnormal bird in other respects, sang occasionally. She had one abortive nest in 1954, in which the eggs were infertile, she half-built one nest in 1955, and in 1956 she made no attempt to nest. She was paired to ♂23 in each year, and relations between them seemed normal. On May 2, 1956 ♂23 was killed and two days later ♀45 spent part of the morning perched high in a tree, singing. The song was rather simple and monotonous in phrasing, but loud and normal in tone. A few days later she was again singing, and the following autumn she was heard to give typical subsong. She was an old bird in 1954, very dark in colour, and was probably suffering from a physiological derangement causing the development of male characteristics. Her potentiality for song had presumably been present earlier, but inhibited from finding expression by the presence of her mate.

The blackbird's other calls are mainly associated with different states of aggressiveness, excitement, alarm or fear. If we follow the current theories of the ethologists and suppose that a bird is motivated by a few simple 'drives' or tendencies, such as the tendency to attack, flee or behave sexually, which can be active either singly or together,[28] we can to some extent relate different calls to different states of balance, or conflict, between these tendencies. Such an approach helps considerably towards an understanding of the blackbird's language. But since I did not study the calls by the strict methods of the ethologist, interpretations in terms of conflicting tendencies must be tentative and I shall rely more on subjective interpretations.

The aggressive 'seee'. This is a very thin, piercing note, lasting for about a second and delivered with the beak slightly open. It must be distinguished from the rather similar, but lower-pitched, alarm 'seee', which is dealt with below. When the circumstances have been known, aggressive 'seee' calls have always been uttered by combative and usually dominant birds in situations connected with the taking up and maintenance of territory. Accordingly, they have been heard mainly from January to June, and again, less often, in October and November. Both sexes utter the note, but males the more often, since they are the more active in territorial behaviour. Typically, the aggressive 'seee' is given by a bird immediately before or after driving away an intruder, by a territory-holder near the border of his territory while watching two other birds in conflict near by (a situation that sounds unusual but is actually rather common, at least where territories are crowded), by one of two more or less equally matched contestants for a territory, between bouts of fighting or posturing, or, finally, by a bird that has recently acquired a territory and asserts itself by this call even when no rivals are at hand. I have never heard it from a submissive or beaten bird. It is the most clearly aggressive of all the blackbird's calls, with little or no escape component.

Chinking. By chinking I mean the metallic and monotonous 'chink chink chink . . .' or 'mik mik mik . . .' which is especially associated with mobbing, going to roost at dusk and leaving the roost at dawn, but is also uttered in many other circumstances. In typical form it is quite distinct from the alarm 'chook, chook' and from the alarm rattle or scream, both of which are dealt with below, though it may gradually change into the former as the bird becomes less aggressive and more nervous, and may break down into the latter at times of great excitement. The chinking of females seems normally to be lower-pitched than that of males.

In terms of the balance of conflicting drives, chinking seems to represent a moderately aggressive tendency combined with a low escape tendency. In subjective terms, a chinking bird is one that is fairly aggressive, hardly or not at all frightened, but inhibited from attacking or able to make only a token attack. As would be expected, chinking may be given in a wide variety of situations.

In territorial situations, a bird may chink when it is either dominant or subordinate to another. For instance, a young male that is persistently trying to establish itself in a territory may, after a few days, begin to chink when he is being chased about by a dominant bird part of whose territory he is trying to annex: earlier he would not do so, and later, when he has finally acquired the territory, he may utter the aggressive 'seee' described above. In the more fluid territorial situations of the autumn and winter, chinking is usually the sign of a dominant bird.

The persistent chinking of blackbirds at dusk is one of the most familiar of autumn and winter sounds. Whenever I have watched this behaviour in known birds, they were established territory-holders or birds who were temporarily dominant in an area. As roosting time approaches, one or two birds start chinking, and before long most of the other territory-holders have joined in. Chinking is most intense in places where good roosting sites attract strange birds from outside the area. The resident birds, chinking persistently, chase and chivvy the intruders, who approach silently and furtively; but eventually they desist and allow the visitors to settle down in their roosts. In territories where roosting sites are few and no visiting birds come, the territory-holders nevertheless usually take up a conspicuous perch and chink for some minutes before going to roost. This evening chinking thus seems to serve as an assertion of ownership at a time when territories are habitually invaded by strange birds.

Chinking accompanying the mobbing of an owl or other large birds requires no special explanation in the light of what has been said above, though why small birds should mob owls at all is another and more difficult question. Mob-bing, almost by definition, is a form of behaviour involving moderate aggressiveness, with inhibition from actual attack. Similarly, when faced by actual or potential nest predators, blackbirds will chink if the threatening animal is too large or formidable to be simply driven away but at the same time does not represent a danger to themselves. It was striking how only those birds which I already knew as the most fear-less would chink when I visited their nests to inspect the young, and this they usually did before or after delivering diving attacks on my head, sometimes while actually attack-ing. Other birds would be silent, or make the 'chook' or alarm 'seee' calls described below.

Chooking. This is the low-pitched 'chook, chook,' made by nervous birds in a variety of situations. It is uttered with the beak closed. Chooking seems to contain no element of aggressiveness. Females often make it if they are watched while prospecting for nest-sites or building, or if they are disturbed from their nests without being unduly alarmed. Any bird may make it in an unfamiliar situation, for instance when searching for food in an enclosed space such as a balcony or back-yard, or in any place which involves an element of insecurity. As mentioned above, chooking may pass into chinking as the bird becomes more excited or aggressive. But the two extremes are so distinct, in sound and in moti-vation, that they are best dealt with as separate calls.

I regard the rather stereotyped and more musical 'pook, pook', typically made when a ground predator threatens the nest or young, as a slightly modified and specialized form of chooking. In gardens it is chiefly elicited by the presence of a cat, especially in the breeding season, and less regularly when a human being approaches the fledged young. Its delivery seems more automatic than that of normal chooking, and it usually continues until the threatening animal has moved away. Fledglings respond at once to this call by keeping silent and motionless and looking around, and especially below them, for the enemy. When I played a recording of the call to young blackbirds taken from the nest when a few days old and raised in captivity, their response was exactly the same.

The alarm rattle. This is the loud chatter, sometimes breaking into a scream, which accompanies moments of sudden alarm, such as when a bird is suddenly surprised at close quarters, or moments of excitement, such as during a hectic but not very serious flight-chase and scuffle. Birds sitting quietly by themselves, especially in autumn on days when chasing is frequent, may give little explosive outbursts of the same sort, suggesting suppressed excitement. Like subsong, this call seems to have no relevance to any other bird but simply to express the feelings of the caller.

The alarm 'seee'. This is a thin 'seee', similar to, but not so high-pitched as, the aggressive 'seee', uttered with the beak slightly open. A few birds in the Botanic Garden—always those that I knew from other evidence to be rather shy—used to give this call when their nests were being inspected. Woodland blackbirds, which are much shyer than garden birds, habitually do so when their nests are approached; indeed this call, heard in woodland from an unseen bird in the trees, is a very good indication that one is near a nest. In a slightly modified form this note is used as the alarm against aerial predators. When a hawk is sighted, blackbirds crouch, with head-feathers flattened down, and give a repeated 'seee, seee, seee . . .', shorter and more regularly repeated notes than those given when the nest is threatened. The same call is often given by the Botanic Garden blackbirds when a carrion crow flies over the garden, especially if it shows any sign of threatening a nest. The stereotyped repetition of this call is probably another example, like that of the 'pook' which silences the young, of how a call in slightly modified form may function as a signal to other birds. It at once alerts all other blackbirds near by.

In subjective terms, the alarm 'seee' is given when a bird, or its nest, is threatened by a specially dangerous or feared predator. It is difficult to interpret this call in terms of conflicting tendencies, as it seems to be without any aggressive element whatever.

Many other small birds have hawk-alarm calls almost identical to the blackbird's. Marler[48] has pointed out that a pure note of this frequency (about 6 kc. per sec.), without clearcut beginning or ending, cannot be located by the hearer, especially if the hearer is about the size of a hawk. None of the three methods by which mammals and birds can locate sound—comparison of the time of arrival of the sound at the two ears, phase difference at the two ears, and difference of intensity of the sound reaching the two ears—can be effectively used. In addition, sounds of this frequency are freely reflected from the branches of trees and other small objects. Marler suggests that this call has been adopted as the hawk-alarm of many different small birds because of all notes it is the one best adapted to give warning without endangering the caller. The evolution of a common call by different species has the further advantage that a bird can receive warning of approaching danger not only from its fellows but from several other species as well.

The flight 'seep'. This is a much lower-pitched note than

either the aggressive or the alarm 'seee'; it is also shorter and has a more clear-cut beginning and ending. There is a faint suggestion of an 'r' sound in it—German authors write it as 'dsirrb', 'sirr', or 'sierr', which suggest the sound better than 'seep' but are not so easily pronounced in English.

Basically this is a flight and flight-intention call. It is often uttered before a bird takes flight to a roosting place, or to a feeding place some distance from its territory, or to any other place which is more than just a few yards away. Doubtless it is as a derivative of a flight-intention call that this note is used in territorial situations by subordinate birds, especially when they are being threatened by a territory-holder. They may take flight immediately afterwards, or they may continue to call for several minutes without flying. At the time of the establishment of territories in early spring, these 'seep' calls, made by nervous-looking birds, with crown-feathers raised and necks upstretched, are among the most characteristic garden sounds.

Territory-holders undoubtedly recognize the subordinate status of such a bird, as they usually approach slowly without posturing, or may even sit quietly near it until it flies off. It may be that it has an 'appeasing' function, in the sense that it inhibits attack, thus ensuring that in encounters in which one bird is clearly dominant over the other, the inevitable result is achieved by the most economical means.

Screaming when handled. When caught by a predator, or, which is equivalent, when handled by man on being trapped, blackbirds give sustained high-pitched screams. This sound at once attracts other blackbirds, which may set about mobbing the predator. Screaming may thus increase the chance that the caught bird is able to struggle free and escape, but I have never seen this happen. The similar screaming of young birds, which begins when they are handled at the age of about nine days, is an extremely powerful stimulus for the parent birds, who call frantically and sometimes mob the intruder. On one occasion the screaming of a nestling which I was handling caused one of the parents to start screaming itself. It also stimulates the other nestlings to leave the nest. At this early stage it thus undoubtedly has value in increasing the chances that some of the young will survive if the nest is attacked.

—6—

Threatening and Fighting

EVERY BLACKBIRD that reaches maturity must threaten and be threatened by other blackbirds, fight and be fought, many times in its life. For this life of constant strife it is equipped not only with beak and claws but with a repertory of postures, which help it to avoid coming to blows by indicating to its antagonist its state of aggressiveness or submissiveness.

These postures are varied, depending not only on the territorial status and immediate aggressiveness of the bird, but also on the status and behaviour of its antagonist. In psychological terms, they seem to depend on both the aggressiveness and the 'confidence' of the bird. Thus an established territory-owner, when being chased out of a neighbour's territory, may retreat silently, or 'chinking', with the head held high and crown-feathers sleeked, while a young unestablished bird or a trespasser from a distant territory will probably retreat in a submissive posture, with the crown-feathers raised, uttering the submissive 'seep'.

When posturing aggressively, blackbirds typically stretch the neck upwards, fluff out the neck-feathers, especially at the back, sleek the head-feathers, and point the beak, slightly opened, above the horizontal. The body-feathers, and especi· ally those of the mantle, may also be fluffed out, so that the whole neck and body is enlarged and the head by comparison appears small. The wings are held stiffly down below the resting position. The tail is usually depressed and slightly fanned (Fig. 4 *top*). Birds in this posture frequently utter the high-pitched aggressive 'seee'. In the most intense forms of this posture the rump-feathers are raised and the tail more markedly depressed and fanned, and the displaying bird may utter the 'strangled song' more often associated with courtship (Fig. 4 *bottom*). The posture then closely resembles the courtship posture and may indeed be indistinguishable from it, though the accompanying behaviour of course differs.

The method of confronting a rival or intruder varies. On the ground, the displaying bird may adopt a moderately aggressive posture and advance towards its antagonist with a jaunty, rolling gait. This is a common method if the other bird is not very aggressive, and is usually sufficient to put it to flight. On a few occasions I have seen a bird, advancing towards or chasing its antagonist on the ground, shake or flick one or both wings as it runs. If the intruder is in a tree, the displaying bird usually hops up through the branches in the typical aggressive posture, but with the head lowered, not approaching directly but weaving up towards the intruder

FIG. 4. *Aggressive postures.*

FIG. 5. *The aggressive 'bow and run'.*

in a roughly spiral course. Occasionally it may stop and wipe its beak on the perch.

If the rival stands its ground, the display may take a more ritualized form. The displaying bird makes little runs, of a few feet each way, up and down beside its opponent. At the beginning of each run the head and tail are lowered, then as the bird moves forward both are gradually raised, until the bird stops with the head fully raised and beak pointing slightly upwards, and the tail raised and slightly fanned (Fig. 5).

In general, the more evenly balanced the antagonists, the more extreme the aggressive posturing. A territory-owner driving out a nervous intruder will probably adopt no special posture. The extreme condition, in which the rump-feathers are raised and the 'strangled song' is uttered, is seen especially in early spring when young males are struggling to establish themselves on disputed ground.

The carriage of the head is the best indicator of the relative aggressiveness of two birds which are in conflict. The more aggressive holds its head higher, with the beak pointing more upwards. The position of the wings and tail, and the degree of fluffing of the body-feathers, are more variable.

Like the aggressive postures, the postures adopted by subordinate or submissive birds are varied. I have distinguished three main types, which for convenience may be called the 'hunched', the 'tail-up' and the 'submissive'. They are not entirely clear-cut, but most of the postures seen can be satisfactorily referred to one of these types.

In the hunched posture (Fig. 6), the head is held low and retracted between the shoulders. This attitude is characteristically adopted by females when they are chased or dominated by males in whose territories they are living in winter, or during the early stages of pair-formation at the end of the winter, but a bird of either sex may adopt the hunched

posture at any time when it is subordinate in a hostile encounter with another bird, and retreating, but not very
alarmed and not intending to take flight. Thus hunched birds

FIG. 6. *The 'hunched' posture.*

FIG. 7. *The 'tail-up' posture.*

may 'chink' as they retreat, and the mantle-feathers may be
raised, as in aggressive display, and apart from the position

of the head and neck the whole attitude and bearing may be that of a moderately confident bird.

Less often, but apparently in very similar situations to those associated with the hunched posture, a striking 'tail-up' posture may be adopted (Fig. 7). The bird runs or hops along with the legs stretched and the tail and whole rear half of the body pointing almost vertically upwards. The plumage may be sleeked, and the chinking note may be uttered. This

FIG. 8. *The submissive posture.*

posture seems to be more readily adopted by males than females. The subjective impression is that the bird is more nervous than when in the hunched posture, and it is consistent with this that the tail may be jerked slightly up and down and the wings flicked, movements which are characteristic of a state of slight alarm.

The most easily recognizable of the postures seen in hostile encounters, and perhaps the commonest, is the one adopted by subordinate or beaten birds and associated with the 'seep' flight-intention call (Fig. 8). The head is held high, with the beak pointing more or less horizontally, and the crown-feathers are raised, giving the head a peaked or crested appearance. The plumage of the neck and body is sleeked, so that the head appears large, the neck thin and the body small—the exact opposite of the appearance produced by the aggressive posture. The outline of the bird, and especially of the head, is so distinct that birds in this posture may be recognized at a great distance. Any bird, male or female, may adopt the posture, but it is most often seen in young males in early spring, when they are trying to obtain territories and are coming into frequent contact with established and dominant territory-owners.

Apart from these special postures that have been described, the wings and tail are sensitive indicators of the mood of a blackbird. Nervous birds, notably trespassers, betray their state by a slight jerking of the tail and flicking of the wings. At the lowest intensity the bird's stance and movements are normal, but the tail is occasionally jerked downwards a little and at the same time partly opened, and then raised more slowly back to its original position. With increasing intensity the tail is held higher and jerked more violently downwards through a greater arc, and the wings at the same time are flicked obliquely downwards and outwards. If the bird remains silent these movements indicate increased nervousness, but when a bird chinks at the same time its condition appears, in psychological terms, to approach a state of general excitement. Loud chinking and violent flicking of the wings and jerking of the tail are the well-known signs of mobbing behaviour, which probably represents the acme of aggressive excitement.

Occasionally, in apparently the same kind of situation as those eliciting wing- and tail-flicking, blackbirds partly open the wing at the wrist while keeping it folded against the body, so that the primaries are separated. I have once seen this follow-ed by wing-flicking, but usually the wings are held motionless in this position. It could be regarded as the lowest intensity of wing-flicking, a preparatory state before the movement itself is produced; but since it is not accompanied by jerking

FIG. 9. *Blackbirds squatting between bouts of fighting.*

of the tail, which normally starts before the wings are flicked, it seems more likely that it represents a psychologically different state.

When both birds are highly aggressive and neither will yield, they fight. Minor clashes may develop over feeding places at any time of the year, but most of the serious fights that I have seen have occurred from February to April. At this time males are competing for territories and females are competing for males. A few serious fights have also been seen during the resurgence of territorial behaviour in autumn.

A typical fight starts with both birds facing each other and one making a sudden attack. The two birds clash with beak and claws, and rise fluttering up to a height of two or three feet before falling back to the ground. On landing they may separate and crouch, or squat, near each other, with beaks open and tails widely fanned, before engaging in another clash (Fig. 9). Or they may remain interlocked on the ground, pecking and clawing at each other, until the bird that is undermost and getting the worst of it eventually struggles free and retreats. Serious fights may continue for many minutes until one bird is beaten and retires. Usually little damage is done, in spite of the violence of the fighting, but it is not rare for one bird to kill the other (see page 155). I have never seen this myself, but perhaps I spoiled my own chance, as once, when a ringed female in which I was especially interested was having a very bad time in a fight with another female, I ran up and separated the birds.

Tail-fanning is the most conspicuous element in postures connected with fighting. It has been mentioned that between clashes birds adopt a squatting posture with beak open and tail fanned. When, as often happens, a dominant bird makes aggressive rushes at another, which evades them at the last moment but, being itself moderately aggressive, does not retreat, the attacked bird usually fans its tail more than the attacker. The attacker may fan its tail slightly only at the actual moment of assault: the attacked bird is more likely to keep its tail more or less fanned all the time, spreading it out to the fullest extent at the moment of avoiding attack. The tail is not depressed, as in aggressive postures and courtship, but is held at the normal level or slightly above it. The attacked bird usually crouches at the moment of attack, then darts away, often zigzagging and making convulsive and rather uncoordinated wing-beats as it does so.

When neighbouring territory-owners are firmly established, encounters between them are usually reduced to formalized patrolling at or near their common boundary. The birds, in moderately aggressive postures, may either run backwards and forwards, each moving alternately and keeping to the side on which its territory lies, or they may make more complicated manoeuvres, especially if there is some cover, such as plants in a flower-bed, breaking the continuity of the surface. They may then run round in circles, constantly turning about and jockeying for position, each still keeping more or less to the side on which its territory lies. Manoeuvring of this kind is commonest between males, but females may take part. Neighbours often make a habit of patrolling along certain limited parts of the common boundary.

At places where three or four territories meet, all the owners may come together for these ritualized manoeuvres. Such gatherings become even more spectacular when young males are trying to establish themselves. They tend to obtain footholds at the junctions between territories, probably because they are not at such a clear disadvantage in such places, and frequently, in early spring when the situation is still fluid, two or more young males show a preference for the same place. Thus eight or more birds may be engaged in manoeuvring and aggressive displays within a few square yards, and all manifestations of aggressive behaviour may be seen, from ritualized patrolling to fights.

Here I must digress to deal with what has been taken to be a special form of display in blackbirds, of unknown significance. Several ornithologists have described 'communal displays', 'social displays', or, as they have sometimes been called, 'spring gatherings' of blackbirds. Others, who have watched blackbirds closely,[31, 44] do not mention them. It has been suggested that these communal displays are in some way analogous to the lek displays of blackcock and other game birds. Communal displays have been recorded from early winter to spring, mainly in early spring. Usually several males have been involved, and sometimes one or two females, which take little part. The postures and movements are often highly formalized, but those that have been described in detail are clearly aggressive.[43, 71, 72] None of these accounts suggests any connection between communal displays and pair-formation.

Some of these displays seem without doubt to be examples of the complex and highly formalized border patrolling of the kind described above, at places where three or more territories meet, with in addition one or more young males present. Many such displays which I have seen in the Botanic Garden might readily have been interpreted as communal or social if the identity of the displaying birds had not shown that they were in fact strictly territorial. Other communal displays cannot be interpreted in this way. They are described as taking place at dawn or dusk, often near places frequented for a special purpose, such as a group of bushes where several birds roost, or drinking and bathing places. I have seen one such communal display in late afternoon alongside a group of bushes in rather open country near Oxford, but never in the Botanic Garden, where cover is well distributed.

I believe that these displays develop, in the first place, when several birds, usually males, come together for some other purpose at times of the year when their aggressive impulses are high. The displays may persist as long as the conditions bringing the birds together persist, become strengthened through habit formation, and, like most blackbird displays, develop into a ritual, finally appearing to be indulged in for their own sake. Thus Dr Bruce Campbell tells me that in early autumn a communal display often takes place at dawn on his lawn, and that while most of the birds taking part appear to have come from roosts beside the lawn, others may fly in from a distance and join in. In this case it seems that it is the rich food supply provided by the lawn, in an area where there is little other mown grass, that is responsible for bringing the birds together in the first place.

Of course the division of these displays into two types need not be a strict one. For instance, if a communal display develops near a roosting place which forms part of one or more territories, some of the participants will be behaving territorially, while others, which have come to roost from a distance, will also be behaving aggressively, but without reference to territory. There may also be a closer link between the two types, for I have found in a few cases in the Botanic Garden that young birds try to take up territories near the place which they have earlier chosen for their winter roost.

All these manifestations of aggressive behaviour are, of course, closely linked to the bird's annual cycle. In order to gain a more exact idea of the changes in aggressive behaviour throughout the year than could be provided by casual observation, I made a note of every aggressive encounter seen, when something was known of the circumstances. These encounters I divided into the following main categories:

(1) One bird clearly dominant over the other, causing it to retreat; usually connected with territory, less often with pair-formation and food.

(2) Two birds patrolling at the border between their territories, more or less equally balanced.

(3) Fights.

Category (1). Aggressive encounters of this type between males, which are almost always connected with territory, are a good indication of the strength of territorial behaviour at any time of the year. As Fig. 10*a* shows, the seasonal variation is very marked, with a main peak in March, as would be expected, and a subsidiary peak in November, corresponding to the autumn resurgence of territorial behaviour. 58 per cent of all these encounters were between old and young males, and in 91 per cent of these the old male was dominant. This is because for half the year, from autumn to early spring, most young males are not established and are continually trespassing in the old males' territories.

By contrast there is comparatively little aggressiveness between males and females shortly before and during the breeding season, and a third of the encounters between the

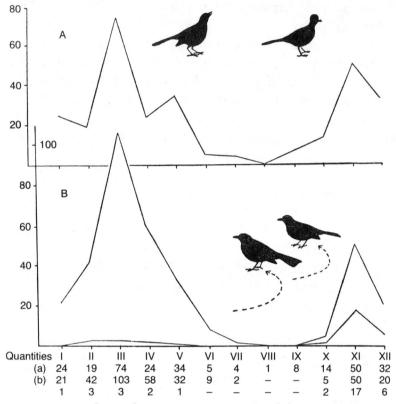

FIG. 10. *Seasonal variation in aggressive behaviour.* (a) *Encounters between males, one driving away the other.* (b) *Patrolling: upper line, all records; lower line, between birds of the opposite sex.*

sexes recorded at this time were not territorial but were between paired birds, an aspect of aggressive behaviour that will be dealt with in a later chapter. Males and females come into conflict mainly in the autumn. This appears to be due to the fact that in autumn the old territory-holders are aggressive to intruders irrespective of sex, while as the breeding season approaches they confine their aggressiveness more and more to members of their own sex.

Category (2). The seasonal variation in patrolling (Fig. 10*b*) is very similar to that for aggressive encounters between males described above. Females are much less active than males. Nearly all (96 per cent) of patrollings recorded in the first half of the year were between birds of the same sex, but from October to December birds seem to patrol indiscriminately with their neighbours of either sex.

Category (3). Fights were classified as 'normal' or 'violent', violent fights being protracted struggles in the course of which the birds lay on the ground interlocked. Most fights are between birds of the same sex, males fighting much more often than females. The seasonal distribution of fights between birds of the same sex is very like that of other aggressive encounters between birds of the same sex. In March, the month when fights are most frequent, three out of twenty-one fights between males were violent, compared with five out of nine between females. Thus, although females fight less often than males in spring, they probably fight more violently, as other observers have noticed. This is probably connected with the different objects of their fights: males fight for territories, females mainly for mates. In every case where I knew the circumstances fully, violent fights between females were between birds which had previously been associating with the same male.

Unlike the fights between birds of the same sex, about the same number of fights were recorded between birds of the opposite sex in autumn as in spring. Four of these were violent, whereas no violent fights were recorded between birds of the same sex at this time.

Thus the records of aggressive encounters in each of the three categories show that there is more aggressiveness between birds of the opposite sex in autumn than in spring. This is not surprising. Aggressiveness is shown towards rivals, whether competitors for territories, for mates or for food. In autumn, when sexual behaviour is very low, a bird may be just as much a rival whether of the same or of the opposite sex.

7

Sexual Displays

THE FULLY developed courtship behaviour of the male is the blackbird's most striking display. The head, with the crown-feathers partially erected and the beak open, is stretched forward; the neck-feathers are compressed, and the body-feathers fluffed out, especially the feathers of the rump, which form a conspicuous hump; and the tail is fanned and depressed. The displaying bird has a curiously wild, staring appearance (Fig. 11). In this attitude the male parades or postures before the female. If both are on the ground, the male typically bows his head, takes a few steps forward, bows again and, turning, repeats his run forward; or he may make more excited movements, jumping up and twirling round between the movements forward. His little runs are usually

FIG. 11. *Male courting an impassive female.*

oblique, to one side of the female, not directly towards her. The whole time, with his beak held open, he usually utters a low 'strangled' song, made up of chattering alarm notes, rough warbles and subdued snatches of what sounds like true song. If the display is performed in a tree, the male remains stationary or at most occasionally shifts to another perch near by, while the bowing part of the display is more prominent, developing into a rhythmic up-and-down movement of the whole head and neck. At the bottom of the bow he may deliberately touch the perch with his beak, a movement reminiscent of the beak-wiping seen in aggressive displays.

The courtship posture may be adopted in flight. The male

then usually flies with very slow wing-beats from perch to perch near the female, often uttering the strangled song. Unmated males may do this even when no female is near, just as they sometimes go into mild courtship postures when they are singing.

As has been mentioned, various features of courtship display are similar to high-intensity aggressive displays, particularly the open beak, the strangled song, the ruffled body-feathers and the bowing and running forward. Indeed, displays of this kind, especially those seen in late winter when females may be either territorial rivals or potential mates, are very difficult, or impossible, to classify as aggressive or sexual unless the circumstances of the birds are known and their subsequent histories followed. Apart from some doubtful cases of this sort, I have recorded courtship displays only from January to June, mostly in February and March.

Courtship displays are associated with pair-formation. They are, however, comparatively infrequent, and in many instances I saw no displays at all between pairs which I watched a good deal during the time of their formation. Nor do males display only to their future mates; in fact, among the individuals I have known, displays have been directed more frequently towards other females. For example, ♂6, an old bird who had lost his mate at the end of the previous breeding season, was seen courting females three times between February 13 and 23, 1954. He became paired to a young female, ♀26, during the first few days of this period. The female which he courted on February 13th may have been ♀26 herself (she was not ringed until the next day), but on February 22nd and 23rd he displayed to two other females while ♀26 was absent. It seems that the initial courtship of the female to which the male becomes paired is usually very brief. If her reactions to the display and her other behaviour to the establishment of the pair-bond, the male's relation to her, presumably based initially on conflicting sexual and aggressive tendencies, no longer expresses itself in courtship posturing. But his relation to other females is still in the courtship stage.

When breeding has begun, paired males sometimes court trespassing females while their mates are on the nest. But most of the courtship display seen at this time is from widowed or unpaired males, which are more numerous than unpaired females (a point that is discussed later, on page 149), and so have to court many females before they can find a new mate.

When they are being courted, females usually sit motionless, apparently unconcerned, or betray slight nervousness by occasional flicking of the wings and tail, or sometimes they hop away. Such behaviour, which is characteristic of early courtship, is probably the usual reaction of unpaired females or those whose pair-bond is not yet firmly established. I have not been able to determine, from the reactions of the female, any means of distinguishing those courtship sequences that are 'successful', in the sense that they later lead to the formation of a pair, from those which are abortive. Paired females, on the other hand, if they are courted, usually attack the displaying male.

The males of established pairs have been seen courting their mates only as an immediate prelude to copulation. The taking up of the soliciting posture by the female, described below, stimulates the male to approach in intense courtship posture, and then to mount. This display usually lasts for only a few seconds, and so is much less conspicuous than the often long-continued displays seen at the time of pair-formation.

If we follow the current theories of animal ethology and interpret the courtship posture as the outcome of a certain balance between sexual, aggressive, and escape tendencies, we might conclude that the initial approaches of a male in breeding condition to a potential mate, and the moments leading up to copulation itself, are associated with an equivalent balance between these conflicting tendencies. But such an interpretation is not satisfactory. The male's courtship posture can hardly be regarded simply as the expression of a

FIG. 12. *Courting male and soliciting female.*

conflict between tendencies that are active from moment to moment: if this was its origin in evolution it has now certainly become emancipated therefrom, and has evolved into an autonomous posture with its own distinctive motivation. For example, a male that is suddenly attacked by a mated female to which he is displaying, will retreat in the full courtship posture, although at the moment of retreating the balance between his aggressive, sexual and escape tendencies must have altered so that the last predominates.

The female appears to initiate copulation by adopting the soliciting posture (Fig. 12), a striking attitude unlike any other of the blackbird. The beak is pointed nearly vertically upwards and the tail is held up at about the same angle. The body-feathers are sleeked, and the legs are well stretched, so that the bird has a slim, attenuated appearance. The beak is usually half opened, and a soft, high-pitched call is sometimes uttered,[73] though I have never been near enough to a soliciting female to be able to hear this myself. In this posture the female runs for a little way in front of her mate, who normally goes into the intense courtship posture and finally mounts. Females solicit copulation for only a short period at the beginning of each nesting cycle: five observed copulations of colour-ringed females took place from one to five days before the laying of their first egg.

The sight of a pair copulating or about to copulate has an immediate and powerful effect on neighbouring males. In nearly every case that I observed, copulations were interfered with by the sudden arrival of one or two males, who either knocked the copulating male off the female or prevented him from mounting. And these attacks have been directed against a territory-holder in the middle of his own territory, where the neighbours normally never go or, if they do, only with every sign of nervousness. Probably because of this habitual interference, copulation is a very brief business lasting only a few seconds. Interferences with copulation are so sudden that it is difficult to decide whether the attacks are evoked by the behaviour of the male or the female. In the stages leading up to copulation it seems probable that the soliciting female is the chief stimulus, since males are not interfered with when posturing equally intensely to an impassive female; but once the male has mounted he appears to be the chief object of the attacks, as has been found in the blackcock[37] and other birds.

Why the tendency to interfere with copulating pairs should ever have arisen is something of a puzzle; it is common to many birds besides blackbirds. It seems pointless and potentially disadvantageous, though not of course to the interfering bird, who may gain by it as his behaviour may tend to keep rival pairs at a greater distance. In any case, the effect does not seem to be serious, as infertile blackbird eggs are not common.

8

Pair-formation and the Pair-bond

THE COURTSHIP displays described in the last chapter are a conspicuous part of the process of pair-formation in early spring, but not, apparently, an essential part. As has been mentioned, the males of some pairs which I watched a good deal at the time of their formation were never seen to display to their mates. Probably the behaviour accompanying pair-formation depends much on the character and status of the male. In many cases, the formation of the pair has been accompanied by more or less persistent chasing of the female by the male, who appears to treat her at first like any other trespasser. When being chased by her prospective mate, the female retreats and avoids his attacks but does not leave the territory. In an extreme instance this chasing was seen over a period of a month, and the male, ♂21, whom I already knew from his territorial behaviour as an extremely aggressive bird, was still attacking her so persistently at the end of March that for some days she was unable to begin to build her nest.

In some cases pair-formation is rapid, especially when a male suddenly acquires a territory on or near which an unmated female is settled, or, later in the breeding season, when a widowed male eventually finds an unpaired female. In other cases it is a gradual process, and it is not possible to determine a precise date after which it may be said that the pair has been formed. This is especially true of the pairs formed in late winter, between a male and a female which have been settled for some weeks previously in the same area, and are then found to be associating more and more closely together without any specific pairing behaviour being seen.

When recording the formation of pairs it is necessary to make certain that birds which appear to be paired really do stay together and breed or attempt to do so. I several times found that apparent pairs were formed during the winter, usually between an old male, who had either lost or was temporarily parted from his mate, and an unattached female. These apparent pairs were mostly short-lived and in any case broke up before the breeding season began; no courtship displays were seen in connection with them. The female came to share the territory with the male and the two birds associated together more or less closely, their exact relationship depending on their mutual aggressiveness. The superficial nature of the relationship was shown when the breeding season approached. Thus in January 1954 one corner of the Botanic Garden held two apparent pairs and an unattached female. A new young male arrived at the end of February and inserted himself between the other males' territories.

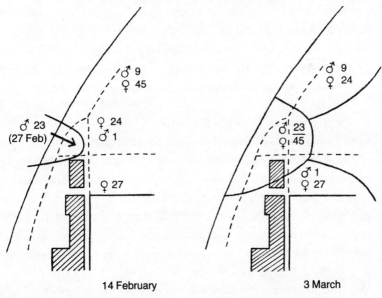

14 February   3 March

FIG. 13. *Changes in partners between three pairs in early.
spring.*

In the confusion that followed, both the apparently paired females shifted and paired with new males (one of them to the newcomer and the other one to the other previously 'paired' male), while the unattached female paired with the remaining male, whose territory had been shifted towards her preferred area by the intrusion of the newcomer (Fig. 13). The pairs thus formed persisted through the breeding season.

I believe that ornithologists who have watched unringed birds have been misled by these apparent winter pairs, and by seeing old pairs associating more closely together after the moult, into supposing that blackbirds normally form pairs in early winter or even autumn. They may occasionally do so, but my records suggest that it is not normal. In the three years 1954–6 the histories of fifty breeding pairs were known in some detail. Sixteen of them were pairs of the previous year of which both members had survived. Of the remaining thirty-four one was formed in January, two in either January or February (probably in January), twenty-three in February and March, seven in April and one in May. Five of the eight late-formed pairs were re-matings after one of the pair had lost a previous mate. Pair-formation was thus confined to the breeding season and the preceding two months.

Once formed, pairs usually stay together for life. Only two of my eighteen colour-ringed pairs of which both members survived from one breeding season to the next broke up, and one of these was exceptional; the female had lost her mate half way through the previous breeding season, and had paired for her second brood with a male that had a territory in a part of the garden which she had never lived in before. When the breeding season was over she gradually moved back to the corner of the garden in which she had first nested, and next season she paired with the male who had taken over her old territory.

While the male is normally dominant over the female before the pair is formed, and may, as mentioned above, be so aggressive to her that he persistently chases her, once the pair-bond is firmly established the female becomes the dominant partner. She can easily supplant her mate from food, and some females habitually do so. The reversal of dominance at the time of pair-formation was most clearly seen in ♂38, a first-year bird, and ♀48, an old bird, in 1955. The pair formed, apparently rather gradually, in the course of February and March. ♂38, an aggressive bird, was frequently seen chasing and chivvying ♀48, and supplanting her from food, and at the end of March, when she was picking at nest-material and showing signs of starting to build, his attacks appeared to be interfering with her efforts. On April 7th they were seen to copulate, and a few minutes later when the male, as was his habit, flew aggressively up to her as she was collecting nest-material, she at once turned and attacked him, whereupon he retreated in the submissive 'tail-up' posture shown in Fig. 7. Thereafter no more aggressive encounters were seen between this pair.

Courtship feeding does not, except perhaps very rarely, occur in blackbirds, but behaviour which is functionally equivalent is common. Especially in the early part of the breeding season when the pair associates closely together, the female often takes food which the male has found, and he abandons it without resistance. Indeed, a single observation suggested that the male may find food specially for the female, though he does not offer it to her. On March 18, 1956, ♂67 and ♀57, a recently formed pair of first-year birds, were feeding a few yards apart out of sight of each other at either side of some low bushes. ♂67 found a large worm, made no attempt to eat it on the spot, but came hopping round the bushes towards his mate with the worm in his beak. ♀57 at once ran towards him and he dropped the worm and stood quietly by while she ate it. The male's behaviour here was very like what is commonly seen when a male is finding food for a nearly independent juvenile: he finds the food, drops it when the juvenile rushes up, and stands by watching as the juvenile eats it.

Old pairs lead a settled existence, with the female mildly dominant over the male but with little aggressiveness on either side. From the end of the breeding season until autumn, especially during the moult, they take little notice of one another. Occasionally females have spent part of the winter away from the territory, and one male did so for a time, feeding for most of the day about a quarter of a mile away from the territory while the female remained sedentary. As the breeding season approaches male and female associate more and more closely together, but I saw no display between old pairs in early spring except for the brief display preceding copulation.

In most birds that normally live in pairs, detailed observation usually brings to light occasional cases of bigamy. In the Botanic Garden I had two cases in the course of four years. In 1953 a young male had two mates, one old and one young. The initial stages of the formation of this trio were not followed, as the females were unringed. A fierce fight between them was seen on March 15th: thereafter they divided the male's territory between them and both had at least one successful nest.

In 1956 the development of a trio was followed in more detail. ♂23 and ♀45 had been paired since 1954, but ♀45 was abnormal (see also page 57)—she nested once in 1954 but her eggs were infertile; in 1955 she half-built a nest, then did nothing further. At the beginning of the 1956 breeding season she showed no signs of nesting. From the end of the previous November ♀55, a young bird, had been frequenting the part of the garden where this pair had their territory. Both ♂23 and ♀45 were aggressive to her. In March she was constantly in or near their territory and ♂23 chased her continually. Rather suddenly, between March 29th and April 1st, ♂23 stopped being aggressive to her, and the three birds were thereafter seen close together, feeding in company. By April 7th ♀55 was dominant over ♀45, occasionally posturing aggressively at her and supplanting her from food. After a few days the two females were found to have divided the male's territory between them, and such aggressive behaviour as was seen between them took place near their mutual boundary. ♀55 started to build a nest on April 12th: ♀45 did not breed. It is reasonable to suppose that ♂23's pairing to ♀55 was in some way caused by ♀45's failure to breed, though relations between them over two previous years had appeared normal.

— 9 —

Nesting

FROM LATE February onwards, mainly in the morning when the weather is mild, the garden blackbirds begin to look for nest-sites. A great number of potential sites may be visited by the prospecting bird, which characteristically hops with deliberate movements through creepers and bushes, stopping, crouching, and apparently testing the suitability of each site, probably the firmness of its foundation and its outlook. This behaviour may continue morning after morning for several days before building begins. Females prospect more often and more thoroughly than males, but males often take part. Sometimes the male simply sits quietly by, watching the female intently, sometimes he joins in, going through the same movements, and sometimes he prospects alone. Because the prospecting bird visits so many sites, I have only exceptionally seen a bird visit and test the site which was finally chosen. Prospecting birds are often nervous, flicking their wings and tail and uttering low 'chooks'. They already show, at this early stage, some of the behaviour connected with the defence of the occupied nest.

It is probable, from her greater assiduity in prospecting, that the female usually chooses the nest-site, but the male may sometimes do so. Sometimes, when both are prospecting together, he is the more active and appears to urge her on, and she may visit a site immediately after the male, as though he had shown it to her. For instance, on one occasion both members of a pair were prospecting in a territory where there was hardly any suitable cover. The male flew to an old woodpecker hole in a birch tree and thrust his head into it, then flew away, upon which the female at once flew over from another tree and also looked into the hole. On another occasion, when similar behaviour was seen in a creeper, the female two days later was building a nest in the site which she had visited immediately after the male, but it was of course not certain that she had not visited the site before the male did so.

After she has been prospecting for some days, the female begins to peck at and pick up nest-material, and shortly after this she begins to build. Males also peck at nest-material and occasionally carry it, but such behaviour is perfunctory. I never saw a male carry the material to the nest or attempt to build.

In the Botanic Garden more nests were built in creepers and other plants trained against the walls than in any other site. Most other nests were in bushes, from three to eight feet above the ground. One nest was built on the ground, on the banks of the Cherwell. While some females built their nests in the same site year after year, others changed sites. Thus ♀7, an old bird (born in 1951 or earlier), nested successfully three times in 1953 in high sites, the last two about 15 feet up on a thickly ivied wall. In 1954, after 12 days of prospecting during which she was seen to visit dozens of sites all over the territory, she built a nest in a completely exposed position four feet up on a wall and within a few feet of passers-by on a busy pavement.

Though prospecting must have the function that it appears to have, that of ensuring the selection of a more or less suitable nest-site, its long duration at the beginning of the breeding season is clearly due to the slow development of the female's readiness to build. New nest-sites for later broods are chosen very quickly and usually little prospecting is seen, even when the female has just moved into a new territory.

At the beginning of the breeding season, nest-building, like prospecting, usually starts in damp, mild weather. Later on, it seems to be less dependent on the weather, but at the end of the season it again depends to some extent on the weather, with the consequence that breeding probably ends on average earlier in dry than in wet years. The first nests of the season are usually built slowly, over a period of a week or two, but later nests may be finished within two days. Late nests are consequently often much less substantially built than early nests. Like the prospecting, the slow building of the first nest is clearly due to the slow development of the breeding behaviour, which becomes active to some extent long before the first eggs are laid. Early in the season building is almost entirely confined to the mornings, and if the weather is cold it may be suspended for days at a time, but later on females often build throughout the day.

The male often accompanies the female when she collects

nest-material, and if, as sometimes happens, she trespasses into neighbouring territories he engages the owning males. This is most often seen when she visits ponds or ditches outside the territory to collect muddy leaves for lining the nest, usually the only necessary material which is not readily available within the territory. If a nest-site has been chosen outside the borders of the territory, the male's conflicts with the neighbouring male are so persistent that the territory is soon extended to include the new site.

The general appearance of a blackbird's nest is familiar to nearly everybody. The bulky cup, of dry grasses, stalks and other suitable vegetable matter, not infrequently supplemented by scraps of cellophane paper in suburban Oxford, is plastered on the inside with mud or muddy leaves, and completed by the addition of an inner lining of fine grass, thin dead stems or rootlets. The mud gives the whole structure great strength and durability. If the first brood is successful the same nest may be patched up, re-lined and used again, and it may be re-used for a third brood. Nests in well-sheltered positions are most likely to be re-used, presumably because they remain in good condition. Nests whose contents have been taken by a predator are not used again, but a new nest may be built only a few feet away.

The eggs, usually three to five in a clutch, are laid daily, usually between about seven o'clock in the morning and noon. Incubation, which lasts about thirteen days, begins gradually while the clutch is still incomplete. The female spends more and more of her time on the nest until, when the last egg has been laid, she is on the nest for about 90 per cent of the daylight hours and all the night. There has been some doubt about the possible share of the male in incubation. In large part this seems to have arisen from the fact that, while only the female normally incubates, the male may go to the nest when she is off and stand guard over it, and may even crouch in the nest-cup, thus giving the impression that he is incubating. However, a few records of males sitting persistently on nests with eggs show that the brooding behaviour is latent in the male and may sometimes be elicited by the prolonged absence or death of the female. Brooding by the male is probably not very efficient as he lacks an incubation patch, the patch of bare skin, richly supplied with blood vessels, that enables the female to apply her body-heat directly to the eggs.

In a few nests I marked the eggs as they were laid, and found that they all hatched in the order in which they were laid. This is to be expected, as the gradual start of incubation means that the first eggs will already have been incubated for a short time when the later ones are laid. But since incubation is only intermittent until the whole clutch is laid, the intervals between the hatching of the eggs are much shorter than the intervals between the laying of them. The whole clutch usually hatches within two days, and often within less than a day. Unhatched eggs remain in the nest indefinitely as long as they are intact.

Both male and female feed the young. The male's contribution is the greater when the young are still small, as the female spends much time brooding them: later their contributions become more nearly equal. The two parents usually keep to a more or less set routine. A common one when the young are small is as follows. As the male approaches the nest with food the female, who has been brooding the young, slips off. The male then feeds the young and departs. A few minutes later the female comes to the nest with food, feeds the young and then settles down to brood them. When the male comes again, she leaves. The male tends to contribute more because he sometimes makes additional visits while the female is off, and the female sometimes returns to the nest without food.

Both male and female take part in the sanitation of the nest, removing the faecal pellets as the nestlings void them and either swallowing them when they are small or, later, flying away with them and dropping them. Dead young also are removed if they are not too large. Once I was lucky enough to be watching at the time. The female visited the nest, fed the young, and then flew heavily away with a dead nestling in her beak and dropped it at the edge of the territory. In other cases where I did not actually witness the removal I have found dead nestlings lying at or near the territory border, and in one of these cases I had evidence that the female had removed it. If a nestling dies after the age of about nine days it is too large to be removed and remains in the nest.

The young normally leave the nest at the age of about thirteen days. They show fear at the age of about seven days, when their feathers begin to grow. At first, if alarmed, they crouch silently in the nest, but at about nine days they begin to scream when handled, and, a little later, handling or any other sudden disturbance causes them to leave the nest prematurely. This behaviour is infectious, the screaming of one young bird causing the others to start scrambling out of the nest. Once they have begun to leave the nest in this way they can only with difficulty be made to settle down again, and though they may appear to become quiet when replaced, they do not usually remain long in the nest. This behaviour certainly has survival value and is not as suicidal as it seems. Once a nest is disturbed by a predator there will usually be no chance at all of survival for those young birds that remain in it, since if all are not taken at once the predator will return later. Thus although young birds that have left the nest prematurely almost certainly have a poorer chance of survival than if they had not been disturbed and had left at the normal time, they are doing the best that can be done under the circumstances. I carelessly caused one family of young blackbirds in the Botanic Garden to leave the nest prematurely, at the age of ten days. They survived well: at least three out of the four were alive eight days later, and two probably survived to independence. Another nest was attacked by a cat when the young were between nine and ten days old. One nestling escaped, and survived to become an adult.

The behaviour of the parents when the nest or young are approached by a human being varies greatly, mainly according to their tameness, or shyness, and their aggressiveness. The degree of tameness of the individual bird does not, as a rule, alter, but its aggressiveness increases as the nesting cycle advances, and is in addition normally greater in females than in males.

Woodland blackbirds, which are usually very shy, often slip silently off the eggs when the intruder is still many yards away, and remain out of sight, either silent or giving the alarm 'seee'. Less shy birds stay longer on the nest, then finally slip off with the 'chook, chook' of alarm. Most of the garden birds are much tamer. One or two of those in the Botanic Garden used to give the alarm 'seee', but most of them would leave the nest more or less reluctantly and remain near by, chooking. A few birds would not leave the nest, and indeed had to be forced off if the contents of the nest had to be inspected. Such birds often peck vigorously at the intruding hand; sometimes they get up off the eggs and, crouching, fluff out the body-feathers, half spread the wings, and snap the mandibles together; then finally, if forced, they retreat to the far side of the nest, still crouching and snapping the beak. Each year I had one or two females that behaved like this, always birds which were known from their other behaviour to be exceptionally tame. The tamest female of all,

♀24, used to return hastily to the nest if she saw me approach-ing when she was off feeding, usually managing to get back before I was able to inspect the contents, and this she would co even when the clutch was incomplete and she was not yet incubating. Repeated interference with the nests of these very fearless birds seemed to have no effect on their tameness at other times. ♀24 would feed her fledged young almost at my feet after they had been some days out of the nest.

As incubation advances, the female becomes increasingly reluctant to leave the nest when disturbed, and at the time of hatching, and when the young are still small, even wood-land blackbirds usually stay on until the intruder is very close. Otherwise their behaviour is the same as it is when they have eggs. As the young become larger, the female becomes more ready to leave the nest but her aggressiveness increases markedly. The tamer females in the Botanic Garden—those that were so difficult to remove from their nests when they were sitting on eggs or small young—sometimes attacked me fiercely when their young were large, repeatedly diving at me, 'chinking' loudly and striking the top of my head with their feet as they swooped past. At times they would inter-sperse this behaviour with what appeared to be a poorly developed form of distraction display, running about on the ground below the nest with the body-feathers ruffled.

Very aggressive females sometimes continue their diving attacks on an intruding human for some days after the young have left the nest; but usually, at this stage, the behaviour of the adults is similar to that shown when a cat or other ground predator approaches: they perch a few yards away and utter the warning 'pook, pook' which causes the young to keep still and silent. As the young become larger and more able to escape from predators, the parents' defence behaviour gradually wanes.

—IO—

Care of the Fledged Young

WHEN there is no external disturbance, the departure of the young from the nest seems to be spontaneous, due to the development of their tendency to move about and perhaps to their attempts to meet the parents when they arrive with food. Probably their mutual disturbance and jostling of each other in the overcrowded nest are often contributory factors. There are reliable accounts which suggest that if one nestling remains long in the nest after the others have left, the parent birds may try to entice it to leave; but I have never seen this myself.

The young are attended and fed by the parents for about three weeks after leaving the nest. At first both parents feed them, but if the female starts to nest again she usually stops feeding them after a few days and begins to build a new nest or repair the old one. The male then continues alone, until, after the young have been about sixteen to twenty days out of the nest, he appears to become less and less willing to feed them. The youngsters continue to beg, sometimes pursuing the male and begging frantically, but gradually they find more and more of their food by themselves and become fully independent. They are not driven away by the male, as is sometimes believed: on the contrary, the male in the latter stages does his best to avoid them, retreating in a harrassed fashion and only occasionally, if persistently importuned, unearthing some morsel and perfunctorily offering it to his offspring. Some males, at this time, alternate periods of attending the young with long periods of singing, especially if their mates are by now incubating their next clutch of eggs.

It is often stated that parent birds are eager to feed any young bird, even one of another species, and many instances have been recorded of such behaviour. Blackbirds, however, rarely feed any young birds other than their own. As I was especially keen to study the survival of young blackbirds after they left the nest, I kept many families of fledged young under daily observation, and recorded only three exceptions to this general rule. Normally the young stay close to the nest for the first few days, but after about ten days they begin to move farther afield. Since the territories in the Botanic Garden are small it frequently happened that after a few days some of the young wandered into neighbouring territories. They then often begged from the neighbouring adults but I never saw a strange adult respond by feeding one of them, even when it was feeding its own fledged young of about the same age. In one striking instance members of two families, one four days and the other eight days out of the nest, had joined company and were perching in the same bush. The male parent of one family and the female of the other were coming with food for them, and though both were begged at vigorously by members of the other family they did not give up their food until they had found one of their own young.

When young birds beg from strange adults, the latter appear flustered, often jumping back a little and sometimes making a perfunctory peck at the strange young, but not attacking it. The young on their part, especially older ones, seem not to beg so whole-heartedly as they do from their parents, as if they know that there is not much chance of their getting any food.

Two of the three instances of birds feeding strange young were rather similar. In both cases a fledgling, very soon after leaving the nest, wandered into the territory of a neighbouring pair who were also feeding young of the same age, and was at once adopted by the male of the pair. The male alone fed it until it reached independence, and it was never seen to be fed by its own parents, although in one case one of the parents was for several days feeding another of its family not more than a few yards away. The third occasion was brought about unnaturally. A fledgling, which had apparently just left a nest outside the Botanic Garden and had been lost by its parents, was put down under the nest of one of the garden pairs which had young just on the point of leaving the nest. While I held it and ringed it near this nest, the female, a very aggressive bird, was attracted by its calls and attacked vigorously. As soon as the young bird was put down she started finding food for it, and since it was very hungry fed it in rapid succession nearly twenty times before it was satisfied and stopped begging. It did not however survive long. These three exceptions to the general rule strongly suggest that the parents learn their own young individually in the first two or three days after they have left the nest.

Not only do adults normally feed only their own young

but I found, more surprisingly, that it is common for the male and female to divide their own family strictly between themselves and not to feed all of them indiscriminately. I did not notice this until 1955, but earlier my method of recording my observations was not precise enough. I first noticed the division of labour between the parents when watching the second, and last, brood of ♂52 and ♀40, a pair of first-year birds. Four young (Red, Blue, Yellow and White) left the nest on May 29th. Almost at once R and Y wandered some way from the nest, to the other side of the garden, where ♂52 fed them. W and B remained near the nest and were fed by ♀40. About fifteen days after leaving the nest the two groups of young started to move about more and approached each other, until on June 16th they were moving about a great deal all over the central part of the garden. But ♂52 continued to feed R and Y, and ♀40 fed W and B. Even when they came close together ♂52 showed no interest in W and B and ♀40 showed none in R and Y, while the young, for their part, followed the movements of the parent which was feeding them intently and did not beg from the other one.

The second observation in 1955 was even more striking. Five young, the second and last brood of ♂9 and ♀24, an old pair, left the nest on June 14th/15th. For the first fifteen days only four of the young were seen, and were always fed by ♀24, so that I concluded that only four had survived and that for some reason the male was taking no part in feeding them. However, on June 30th and again on July 2nd I saw ♂9 with food in his beak, but did not see him feed any of the young. On July 5th I again saw him with food. He flew to a wall and remained there, still holding the food and looking about him. One of the four youngsters came up and begged, rather half-heartedly, and ♂9 flew quickly away without giving up the food, going down to the ground and still apparently looking for something. He then flew back to the wall, near the young one who did not beg again, and soon after I lost sight of him. The whole time another of the four young was near by in full sight but showed no interest in his parent with food. Four days later I again saw ♂9 with food, near one of the four young, who did not beg and was not offered the food. ♂9 was clearly searching for another bird, and after a few minutes found the fifth member of the family, Black, whom I had not seen since he left the nest. Black was clearly well fed and would not take the food which ♂9 kept trying to offer. After several attempts to make Black take the food, and paying no attention to another of the family which had approached and was standing near by, ♂9 at last swallowed the food and flew off. Black, who had had the undivided attention of the male for twenty-five days, apparently never needed to call for food, which was probably why I had never seen him and also why ♂9 found him hard to locate; while the other four had been seen day after day, begging loudly as they pursued ♀24 and were fed by her.

These two families in 1955 were not chosen for detailed observation because of anything unusual in their behaviour, but only because the openness of the part of the garden where they lived and the tameness of the parents made them especially easy to watch. In 1956 I decided to pay special attention to the feeding of fledged young, in order to check the 1955 observations. Unfortunately several broods failed at the end of the season or were unsuitable for other reasons, but such observations as I was able to make confirmed what had been found in 1955. I expected that only the last broods would be divided between the parents in the way described above, since when the female re-nests she usually stops feeding the previous brood after a few days; the male must thus normally take over the care of the whole family from then onwards. However, while this was the general rule, there were two cases where the female, although she re-nested, took sole charge of one of the previous family and fed it until it was independent. In one case she re-lined the old nest and laid the first egg of her new clutch when the youngster had been out of the nest for fifteen days and was nearly independent. In the second case the female began to build a new nest when the youngster which she was feeding had been out of the nest for only four days, laid her first egg four days later, and continued to look after the youngster for at least another eight days, regularly coming off the eggs to feed it. In neither case was the division of labour necessitated by the large size of the family. The male of the first pair was feeding only one of his own family and one adopted from a neighbouring pair (one of the exceptional cases mentioned above), while the male of the other pair was also feeding only two young ones. In 1956, as in 1955, I found that youngsters which were being fed by only one parent ceased to beg for food from the other.

It is easy to see how the young may become conditioned to either the male, a black bird, or the female, a brown bird, but it is less clear how the parents learn to distinguish, as they certainly do, between the individual young. In the first few days after the young have left the nest, when they are still relatively immobile, the parents clearly learn where their young are hiding and search for them there. It is presumably at this stage that they begin to recognize the young individually and the division of labour between the parents develops. Later, when the youngsters are ranging widely over the garden and the parents are still feeding the same ones, paying no attention to the others, they probably recognize them as we recognize other human beings, by their individual appearances and their voices.

Of the families which were divided strictly between the two parents in 1955 and 1956, four young birds were later seen when they had assumed their first-winter plumage. Three were males, and had each been fed by the female parent, while the fourth, a female, had been fed by the male parent. This sample is, of course, too small to be more than suggestive.

This behaviour was entirely unexpected, not having been described, so far as I know, in any other passerine bird. It is unlikely to be unique, but most of the smaller passerines are very difficult to observe closely during the post-fledging period. Division of the family between the two parents is regular in some grebes.[62] It is difficult to see how the behaviour can be adaptive: indeed it seems potentially disadvantageous, since if one parent is killed the other will be less ready to take over the whole family than it would be if it had previously been feeding all of them indiscriminately.

---II---

The Young Bird grows up

AS SOON as the young blackbird leaves the nest, barely able to fly and with only a stump of a tail, it seeks cover, usually a little above the ground, and spends most of its time sitting motionless. It occasionally utters a subdued cheeping, which becomes louder and shriller when it begs. This call seems to be simply a louder version of the cheeping notes which are made in the nest. In addition, it begins to utter a call never heard in the nest, an incisive single or double 'chuck' or 'chuck-uck', with many variants, which is repeated at intervals when the young bird is alone and enables its parents to find it among the thick cover in which it is hiding. This note has the characteristics, described by Marler,[49] of a call which can easily be located. It is staccato, containing hard consonant sounds, and has a wide range of pitch; it is in fact the very opposite of the alarm 'seee'.

After about a week the young bird begins to venture into the open, often hopping out to meet the parent as it approaches with food or pursuing it out into the open after being fed. Its flight is weak for the first few days, but by about the eighth day after leaving the nest it can fly strongly and may perch high in trees and bushes. After about two weeks young birds regularly range widely over their parents' territory and beyond, but they constantly return to it, especially when they are alarmed. It is not until about twenty days after leaving the nest, when they become completely independent, that they finally leave their parents' territory.

The two calls heard soon after the young leave the nest persist but are modified as the young grow older and move about more. The begging call, which originates as a soft cheeping and then grows louder, becomes the most frequently uttered call, developing into a loud, insistent shrilling; while the 'chuck-uck', which is now losing its function of enabling the parent to find the young, becomes rather variable and develops into a variety of staccato phrases, 'chuck-uck-uck', 'zeek-zeerk', etc., of varying pitch but with the first note usually higher-pitched than the others. At about the time that the young become independent, other notes develop, especially the flight 'seep' and a variety of warbling and chuckling notes which are often uttered by young birds sitting by themselves and are reminiscent of subsong.

The begging behaviour of young blackbirds is typical of young passerine birds. The bird stretches its head forward to the fullest extent, utters the shrill cheeping with beak widely open, and vigorously flutters its half-spread wings. When it is standing to one side of the parent the wing on the side away from the parent is fluttered violently while the other is hardly moved.

About seven days after leaving the nest the young start

pecking at possible food-objects. Much of this early food-testing is clearly a trial-and-error process: the birds peck at daisies, bits of soil, twigs and such things, and sometimes jump up and peck at flowers and leaves a foot or two off the ground. Bright and shining rounded objects seem to attract them. A juvenile in captivity showed immediate interest in cherries, which it could never have seen before, in polished shoes, and in snail shells. With an inborn interest in such objects it is easy to see how young blackbirds are initially attracted to the many kinds of fruits, which form a large part of their diet soon after they reach independence.

At the same time the more specialized feeding movements, characteristic of the species, begin to be shown. Young birds begin to dig in leaf litter and soil ten days after leaving the nest, with the synchronized flicking movement of the beak and scratching movement of the foot fully developed. I have seen large worms pulled out of the ground, shaken, and eaten by young birds thirteen days after leaving the nest.

Towards the end of the dependent period young birds show alternating juvenile and adult behaviour. After a spell of finding food for itself more or less successfully, a youngster will suddenly stop, look up, and uttering loud begging notes hop off in search of a parent. When being fed by the parent, even as long as twenty days after leaving the nest, it may hardly react at all to a piece of worm which the parent lets fall to the ground, perhaps pecking at it perfunctorily but making no attempt to eat it until it is offered in the parent's beak. A few minutes later it will again be searching for food and dealing with it almost as expertly as an adult.

It has already been mentioned that the parents do not drive the young away when they become independent. The movement away from the territory, which is usually sudden, seems to be due to the search for suitable feeding areas. Occasionally juveniles have not moved away at this stage, and after they have done so they often return for short periods without interference. Strange adults are usually tolerant of these recently independent juveniles; they rarely attack them and then only perfunctorily. Indeed juveniles, which become aggressive at an early age, have been seen just as often attacking adults. Even in its own territory an adult, when thus attacked, usually retreats in a harrassed fashion. There seems little doubt that some characteristic of the juvenile, possibly the spotted plumage, inhibits the adults' aggressive behaviour.

Towards each other juveniles show both social and aggressive tendencies. Young from different families may associate together even while they are still being fed by their parents, and independent juveniles are even more sociable. At the same time they are aggressive: from the age of eleven days after leaving the nest I have seen juveniles attacking each other, pecking and making aggressive rushes, and I have seen them fight after sixteen days, clashing and fluttering up together into the air. These conflicting tendencies, social and aggressive, persist for several weeks. Thus I watched two large juveniles, one six and a half weeks out of the nest and the other of unknown age, keeping company together for some time. They ranged widely over the garden, coming into contact with adult territory-owners who threatened them a little, stopping to feed together, and flying on together. Several times one was seen to attack the other.

I had a little evidence that some attachment between young of the same family may persist for weeks after they have left the nest. There is so much movement among juveniles at this time that the likelihood of seeing two birds of the same family together by chance is difficult to evaluate, but on a number of occasions, from late summer to mid-winter, I saw two young birds of the same family together after days or weeks during which I had seen neither of them.

In late summer and autumn young blackbirds indulge in a form of behaviour which might perhaps be called 'play', though, as will be seen later, it cannot always be separated from the incipient sexual behaviour which is seen chiefly in October. Play typically consists of apparently purposeless, and often excited, behaviour in relation to twigs, leaves and other small objects which the bird comes across. As an example the behaviour of ♀58, a young bird, may be described. On September 11, 1955, she was watched dashing round in small circles for several minutes in a flower-bed. She would make a frenzied rush, then stop, pick up a leaf and hold it for a few seconds in her beak, drop it, and rush on, keeping to the same few square yards. Occasionally she uttered subdued alarm rattles. For part of the time another young bird was standing very near, but took no part and did not seem interested. This example, one of many, is typical of the kind of behaviour involved, and in showing that it is not directed towards and has little effect on other birds.

On fine days in autumn there is a great deal of chasing between young birds, especially when they are feeding communally on fruit trees. Wild flight chases develop in which young males most frequently chase other young birds of both sexes. These chases seem simply to be the result of the two conflicting tendencies we have already noted, the aggressiveness of the young birds and the sociability which brings them together: they are not connected with either territory or pair-formation.

In late September and October, especially on mild sunny days, young birds show incipient breeding behaviour. Females prospect for nest-sites and collect and carry about nest-material, but I have never seen one actually build a nest;

young males too may pick up and carry nest-material. I once saw a young female show typical soliciting behaviour and a young male go through typical copulatory movements with a stick. In this last case the male's behaviour was very like autumn play. He kept on picking up the stick, jumping back excitedly and then dropping it. Three times, after dropping it, he squatted on it, depressing the tail, fluffing out the belly feathers, and raising and fanning the wings as if balancing. Perhaps all 'play', as in this case, represents the early manifestations, often in incongruous circumstances and more or less distorted, of innate activities that will become functional later. Old birds engage much less, or not at all, in these autumn activities that are such a large part of the life of young birds. Only occasionally do they take part in the autumn chasing. I have not seen them 'playing', and the only sign of breeding behaviour that I have seen is occasional prospecting for nest-sites. Subsong in autumn is also heard more often from young birds than from old.

The most precocious young birds establish territories in autumn. This important step in the bird's life, which may perhaps be regarded as the first mark of its adult status, has already been dealt with in an earlier chapter.

———— 12 ————

The Dispersal of the Young

WHEN THEY wandered away from their parents' territory on gaining independence, most of the young blackbirds born in the Botanic Garden did not move far. I often saw them feeding one or two hundred yards away from their birth-place, and occasionally young birds would revisit their parents' territory for short periods in autumn or early winter. I was of course more likely to see those which stayed close at hand than those which moved farther afield, but ringing returns supported my observations: none of the considerable number of young birds born in the Botanic Garden and found dead in June, July and August was more than two miles from its birth-place.

Of just over four hundred birds that I had ringed as nestlings in or near the Botanic Garden I found thirty-one breeding in subsequent years. Twenty-five of these were within 800 yards of their birth-place and the farthest was two and a quarter miles away. Males and females dispersed about the same distances. Here, too, I was likely to find those that moved the shortest distances, but again ringing returns confirm that young blackbirds do not as a rule breed very far from where they were born. Werth[78] found that 93 per cent of British blackbirds ringed as nestlings and recovered in subsequent breeding seasons were within five miles of their birth-place, 72 per cent being found 'where ringed'. Since I probably found all of my nestlings which subsequently bred 'where ringed', but only a small proportion of those that bred more than a mile away, my thirty-one birds probably represented about 75–80 per cent of the total surviving.

Each year I trapped and ringed a few young birds which had wandered into the Botanic Garden soon after they had become independent. These birds had almost certainly come from nests a short distance away, as was indicated by the presence among them of a few that I had ringed as nestlings in neighbouring gardens. Of twenty-six such birds, trapped from late June to early August, I later found thirteen breeding. Eleven of them were within 200 yards of where I had trapped them and the other two were within 400 yards. Three others were known to be alive in the following breeding season: one of them was probably trying to establish himself near where he had been trapped, but died before he had succeeded; the other two probably bred within a few hundred yards of where they had been trapped, as they occasionally trespassed in the Botanic Garden. Thus within a few weeks of gaining their independence these juveniles had chosen the area where they were to spend the rest of their life as adults.

The Dispersal of the Young

Round the area which they have chosen as their home, the juveniles move about over a few hundred acres during the autumn and winter. In autumn they collect in loose flocks and exploit the different fruit trees as they ripen. Later, when the fruit is finished, these loose flocks move on to playing fields and rough grassland, or, in cold weather, break up as the individual birds seek food in sheltered places under trees and hedges. In October and November 1955, for instance, 26 different juveniles born in or near the Botanic Garden (11 males, 15 females) visited part of the garden where there was a heavy crop of *Crataegus* and *Sorbus* fruit, and with them were many other unringed juveniles. Later, when this fruit was finished, some of the same birds were seen feeding in Christ Church and Magdalen Meadows, and a few were seen further afield, for instance on New College Sports Ground half a mile away.

Some of the young birds in these flocks would also be territory-holders. As we have seen, young birds that establish territories in autumn and early winter usually spend only part of the day in them, mainly the early morning, and join a flock for the rest of the day.

I used to see approximately an equal number of males and females among the colour-ringed juveniles that I found in the flocks in early autumn, but later, from November to February, I saw nearly twice as many males as females. This was, I think, not because some females moved away during the winter, but was the result of the females' tendency to become more sedentary than the males as winter advances. I used often to find females in the same circumscribed area day after day, whereas males, ranging more widely, were seen in a greater number of different places but less often in each place. Males were thus more likely to be seen occasionally even if their preferred areas were some distance from the

Botanic Garden. By March, when most of the breeding territories were established, I again saw equal numbers of males and females.

Generalizations based on the variable behaviour of a number of individual birds lack some of the interest of the indi-

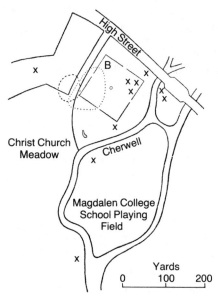

FIG. 14. *Recorded movements of ♂27 during his first autumn and winter. B: birthplace 1954. Crosses: observations September–December. Dotted line: observations in January. Broken line: breeding territory in 1955.*

vidual histories. The following short accounts of the movements and settling down of three males and three females illustrate some of the points touched on in this chapter, as well as a few of those dealt with in earlier chapters.

♂27 (Fig. 14)

Born in the Botanic Garden, leaving the nest on April 25, 1954. As a juvenile seen regularly up to June 20th, in parents' territory till May 20th then in other parts of the garden and on a playing field 300 yards away. Seen only twice in July and not at all in August. From September to December seen in several places, up to 500 yards from its birth-place; moult to

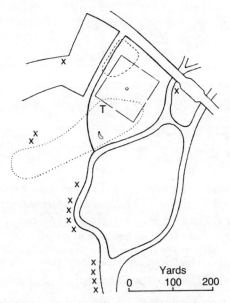

FIG. 15. *Recorded movements of ♂28 during his first autumn and winter. T: where trapped, July 1954. Crosses: observations September–December. Dotted line: Observations January–March. Broken line: breeding territory in 1955.*

first-winter plumage complete on September 21st. In January 1955 tending to settle at one side of the Botanic Garden, and by the end of January established in a territory just outside the garden, 100 yards from its birth-place.

♂28 (Fig. 15)

Trapped as an unringed juvenile in the Botanic Garden on July 5, 1954. Seen subsequently in July in the same place, then not again till September 21st. From September to December seen a dozen times feeding on fruit (mainly hawthorn) in several places, up to 550 yards from the trapping place. From January to March 1955 seen several times in or

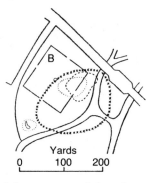

FIG. 16. *Recorded movements of ♂31 during his first autumn and winter. B : birthplace 1954. Crosses : observations September–January. Dotted line : observations in February. Broken line : breeding territory in 1955.*

near the Botanic Garden, apparently trying to settle near where trapped. On April 3rd suddenly occupied a territory about 100 yards from where trapped, on the death of the previous owner.

♂31 (Fig. 16)

Born in the Botanic Garden, leaving the nest on July 13, 1954. Seen regularly up to the end of July, in or near its parents' territory, then not again till August 30th. Seen about twenty-five times from September to February, always in or just outside the Botanic Garden and showing a preference for one side of the garden. All observations within 200 yards of birth-place. From early February 1955 trying to establish himself in ♂6's territory, but did not succeed until March 13th when ♂6 died.

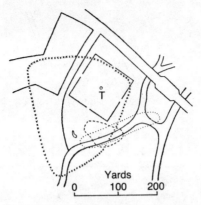

FIG. 17. *Recorded movements of ♀55 during her first autumn
and winter. T: where trapped, July 1955. Crosses: observations December–January. Broken line: breeding territory in
1956.*

♀55 (Fig. 17)

Trapped as an unringed juvenile in the Botanic Garden on
July 5, 1955. Seen subsequently in July, August and early
September near where trapped: moult to first-winter plum-
age complete on September 5th. Seen many times from late
September to January 1956, showing a preference by early
December for the side of the garden where she later settled.
No observations in late January and February. Throughout
March persistently along the same side of the garden and just
outside, often chased by established birds. Associating with
♂23 at the end of March and by April 1st paired with him
(forming a trio as he was already paired with ♀45).

♀61 (Fig. 18)

Born on the edge of Magdalen Meadow, leaving the nest
about April 27, 1955. Immediate post-fledging movements
not followed, but seen near where born on May 11th, and on

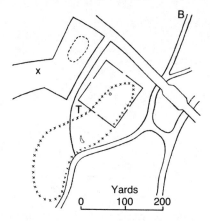

FIG. 18. *Recorded movements of ♀61 during her first autumn and winter. B: birthplace 1955. T: where trapped, July 1955. Crosses: observations September–January. Broken line: breeding territory in 1956.*

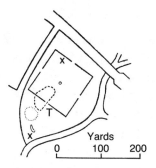

FIG. 19. *Recorded movements of ♀74 during her first autumn and winter. T: where trapped, July 1955. Crosses: observations October–November. Dotted line: territory occupied 4th December 1955 to 8th January 1956. Broken line: breeding territory in 1956.*

June 6th in the Botanic Garden 300 yards from birth-place. Trapped in the Botanic Garden on July 8th. Moulted into first-winter plumage by August 29th. Seen several times from late September to mid-January 1956, in and a short distance outside the garden, up to 550 yards from birth-place. Settled in a territory and paired by late February, 300 yards from where born and less than 200 yards from where trapped in July.

♀74 (Fig. 19)

Trapped as an unringed juvenile in the Botanic Garden on July 7th, 1955. Seen again in July and retrapped near by. Not seen again until October 2nd. Only once seen in November. By December 4th established in a small territory by itself and regularly in it until January 8th, 1956, driving out intruders. Abandoned this territory in February. Paired with ♂79 by early March in a territory less than 50 yards from where trapped on July 7th, 1955.

⸺ 13 ⸺

The Breeding Season

GARDEN BLACKBIRDS usually lay their first eggs in the middle or at the end of March, and their last eggs in May or June. Occasional birds start a good deal earlier than this and continue later. In the course of the three months or so of breeding one nesting attempt follows another in close succession. In the Botanic Garden during the period of my study most pairs made two, three or four nesting attempts in the season, the average being 2·7. There are records elsewhere of pairs producing four families in one season, but none of mine succeeded in producing more than three. Four are possible only if the pair starts unusually early or continues unusually late, and has an unbroken run of success. The most prolific of my birds laid twenty eggs in the course of one season, in four clutches (4, 5, 5, and 6), but only two of these were successful, producing eight young. The record appears to be held by a blackbird in Germany that laid twenty-six eggs in one season, in six clutches.[11]

As we have seen, in mild weather females begin to prospect for nest-sites from late February onwards, and especially if the weather is mild they may begin to build soon after; but the first eggs are not usually laid till much later. Myres[53] analysed several thousand British Trust for Ornithology nest-record cards for the blackbird and song thrush for the years 1950–3, and found that in southern England, from about the middle of March, a rise of mean temperature above 40°F. was followed some five days later by a great outburst of laying by these two species. Before mid-March a rise of mean temperature above 40° was followed by few, if any, layings: clearly the birds were not yet ready to respond. A consequence of this response to temperature is that, owing to the variability of the weather in early spring, the time of breeding may vary considerably from year to year. My own much less numerous records for the Botanic Garden are in agreement with Myres' findings.

It is however only the earliest females that are stimulated to lay at this time. The latest of my females did not lay their first eggs until May (Fig. 20). The early females were mainly old birds, the very late ones were all young birds. In some cases the reason for the late start of the young birds was clear, as they had been late in getting paired and settled in their territories. And even those young females that had been paired for some time before they started to nest had usually been settled for a much shorter time than most of the old females, many of which had been with their mates all through the winter.

The date on which the last clutch is started is rather

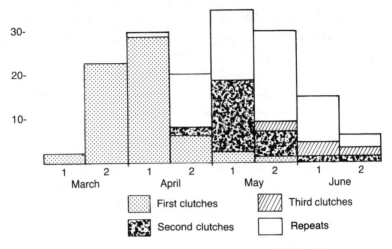

FIG. 20. *The Blackbird breeding season at Oxford. Showing all nestings of 59 pairs over four years. All clutches laid after a previous failure are classified as 'repeats'.*

variable, as it depends much on the timing, and fate, of the previous clutches. If a nesting attempt finishes in late May it will almost certainly be followed by another: if it finishes in early June it will probably be; but a nesting attempt which finishes in mid-June or later is likely to be the last for the season. Thus last clutches may occur at any time from the beginning of May to the end of June. Here again there is a difference between old and young females. Old females tend to go on nesting later than young ones.

It seems probable that wet weather in June may prolong the breeding season and dry weather shorten it, but with the great variability in the dates of the last clutches, due to the timing of the previous nesting attempts, very many pairs of blackbirds would have to be kept under observation in order to demonstrate this. My fifteen to twenty pairs were not enough. The immediate effect of wet weather at the end of the season is, as at the beginning, to stimulate nest-building.

Normally this leads to another full nesting attempt, but in the third week of June 1956, following wet weather, three nests were built in the Botanic Garden and abandoned without eggs being laid in them.

Severe weather in the course of the breeding season may temporarily inhibit laying. In 1952 there was a blizzard at the end of March. Not only were many of the blackbird nests that had already been started deserted, but analysis of the nest record cards showed that for several days virtually no new clutches were started. Three or four days after the blizzard ended and night temperatures rose above freezing point there was a huge outburst of laying. No such catastrophes occurred from 1953 to 1956, but there were long droughts in April 1954 and April 1955. Four pairs of blackbirds in the Botanic Garden appeared to be affected by the drought of April 1954, in that they had unusually long intervals before the start of their second nests, but the drought in 1955 ended earlier and hardly any of the Botanic Garden birds were at a stage when they could be seriously delayed by it. The nest-record cards, however, with their much larger numbers, showed that both droughts had an effect. By April 24th, 1955, the last day of the drought, hardly any blackbirds were starting new clutches, but many began to lay on the 25th and the days following, when a moist westerly airstream put an end to the drought.

The interval between successive nesting attempts is variable. If there is nothing to disturb the birds' normal routine, the laying of the new clutch usually starts from four to ten days after the ending of the previous nesting attempt. It seems to make no difference whether the previous nesting attempt was successful or not. I had no interval shorter than two days, from the time the young left the nest to the time the first egg of the new clutch was laid, but there is a record of eggs being laid in a new nest while the young were still in the old nest.[5] What little evidence there is suggests that such 'telescoped' broods may be commoner in Germany than in Britain.

Young females, with a mean interval of 10·6 days, took on average a little longer to start their new clutches than old females, whose mean was 7·5 days. The difference was mainly due to the fact that several young females had unusually long intervals. Owing mainly to the fact that they started to breed later, and to a lesser extent to the fact that they stopped breeding a little earlier, young females started fewer clutches per year than old females. Old females most commonly started three, less often two or four, the average for eighteen old females being 3·1. Young females started from one to four, most commonly two, the average for sixteen young birds being 2·3.

In each year, breeding started between one and two weeks later in broad-leaved woodland on the Wytham estate, three miles from Oxford, than in the Botanic Garden. Very few woodland nests had eggs in March. From the middle of May onwards it becomes rather difficult to find woodland nests, because of the density of the undergrowth, so that I did not obtain enough accurate information on the end of breeding in woodland to tell whether it was correspondingly later than in the gardens. There seemed no doubt that the droughts of April 1954 and April 1955 had much less effect in woods than they did in gardens. In the wood new clutches were being started in the driest period in both years when few or none were started in gardens. This is of course not surprising, since a drought that is severe enough to parch the open ground of gardens and parks has much less effect on the sheltered woodland floor.

Wytham woods are about one hundred to five hundred feet higher above sea level than Oxford gardens, and so are probably a little colder. The later breeding cannot however be attributed to this difference in altitude, as the Wytham nests were at all levels, from the top of the hill down to the bottom, and each year the earliest nests in a suburban area of gardens on Boar's Hill, near Oxford, which is higher than Wytham, were about as early as the Botanic Garden nests. That blackbirds breed later in woodland than in towns and suburbs is certainly general, and it has long been on record. It has been suggested that the difference is due to better feeding conditions in gardens. But whether they are really better in gardens seems doubtful; this will depend largely on the importance to the birds of the artificial food-supply directly provided by man. Moreover, to be valid the explanation must not depend on the special requirements of blackbirds or any other species, as earlier breeding in gardens than in woods seems to be rather common: it has been found, for instance, in the robin, song thrush, great tit and blue tit. In addition to the possible effects of the food-supply in early spring, several other factors may be involved. Garden birds tend to be more sedentary than woodland birds, presumably because man's activities supplement their food-supply through the hardest part of the winter and enable them to remain in their territories, and so they may be able to respond earlier to the external stimuli which initiate breeding than can woodland birds, which are later in taking up territories and perhaps also in pairing. Added to this, towns are illuminated at night and are noisier than the country, and have a local climate that is a little warmer than the surrounding country, and it is known that an increase of light, increased wakefulness, and warmth can all contribute to the maturing of the gonads of birds and stimulate breeding.

Occasionally blackbirds and other birds start nesting in autumn, if the weather is very mild. 1953 was such a year.

November and December were unusually warm, becoming exceptionally so from the second week of November. A small proportion of the blackbird population started breeding in the second half of November and continued to the beginning of January 1954. Of the thirteen nests recorded for the whole of Britain,[66] young hatched in at least three nests and flew from at least one of them. Unfortunately few of these nests were seen by ornithologists: none of the Botanic Garden birds nested. It would be interesting to know if those that nested were mainly old or young birds. As we have seen, most old birds are paired and settled in their territories, and so are in a better position to breed than the young birds; on the other hand young birds show more signs of incipient sexual behaviour in a normal autumn than do old birds.

Why should blackbirds in England breed from the middle of March to the end of June? Why not from the middle of April to July? In general, birds which feed their young on some special food time their breeding so that their young are being fed when this food is most abundant or most easily obtained. Thus young swifts are in the nest at the time when flying insects are most abundant, young tits when woodland caterpillars are at their most abundant, young starlings when leatherjackets are most numerous, and so on. For blackbirds the situation is not quite so straightforward.

Garden blackbirds feed their young mainly on earthworms, but worms are usually most abundant in March and April, after which their numbers sharply decline. If the worm supply were of critical importance blackbirds would be expected to start breeding earlier. But weather, rather than the abundance of food, seems to be the critical factor at the beginning of the breeding season. Sharp frosts not only make it difficult for blackbirds to find what food there is, but make it dangerous for a female to leave her eggs or young uncovered. Snowfalls are known to cause a heavy loss of nests. We have seen that the onset of mild, wet weather is a powerful stimulus for the beginning of nest-building. Probably, therefore, the start of breeding is timed to coincide with the average time of onset of weather which makes successful nesting possible.

Later, in May and June, when worms become less easy to find, a variety of small invertebrates, especially caterpillars and other larval insects, are fed to the young. For several weeks both weather and food-supply are favourable. Then conditions deteriorate again. By the end of June the flush of insect larvae is past, and the ground is soon parched after a few sunny days, so that worms too are frequently hard or impossible to obtain. In the Botanic Garden and surrounding gardens I found that many nestlings died during droughts at the end of the breeding season, and those that survived were on average lighter than the earlier nestlings. Thus the breeding season ends at a time when, due to the combined effects of weather and a decreasing food-supply, it is becoming increasingly difficult for the birds to feed a family.

──14──

Clutch-size

BLACKBIRDS may lay any number of eggs from two to six in a clutch. Apparently complete clutches of one are recorded occasionally, but most if not all of these are probably the result of the loss of eggs or disturbance of the bird. Clutches of two and six are also rare in England, together amounting to only about 4 per cent of the total.[64]

The average clutch-size rises and then falls in the course of the breeding season. At the beginning of the season three or four is the usual number. Occasional clutches of five are laid as early as the end of March, but five is not common until the second half of April. As the season advances and clutches of five increase, clutches of three become less frequent; fours remain common. The rise continues until just after the middle of May. Thereafter clutch-size begins to fall rather rapidly. Fives have almost dropped out by the middle of June, and by the end of June most clutches consist of three eggs.

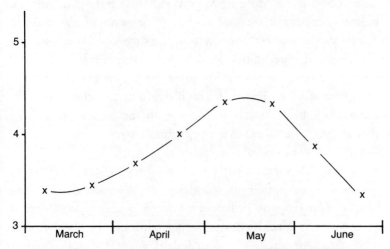

FIG. 21. *Seasonal variation in average clutch-size of Black-birds in southern England. Based on 3,031 clutches in 1950-3.*

The few clutches of six are found during the period when the fives are most numerous, from the end of April to the begin-ning of June.

The hundreds of nest-record cards for the blackbird that have been filled in by members of the British Trust for Ornithology make it possible to examine this seasonal rise and fall in clutch-size in some detail. As Fig. 21 shows, the pattern is very regular when data from several different years are combined. The picture for individual years may be rather different, most of the variations away from the norm being attributable to unseasonable weather at about the time when the clutches were laid. In 1951, for instance, clutch-size in southern England began unusually high, then dropped towards the end of March, instead of rising, then rose at the beginning of April, but dropped again slightly in mid-April. Correspondingly, mean temperatures were high for several days round the middle of March and then fell, with minima below freezing on several nights at the end of the month. There was a marked rise in temperature on April 1st, and this rise continued until the 6th, when temperatures fell and remained low for about five days. In 1952 clutch-size fell exceptionally low just after the blizzard at the end of March, the average being nearly half an egg lower than is normal for that period. In 1954 and 1955 clutch-sizes were unusually low towards the end of the droughts in April.

Clutch-size varies a little according to habitat. Each year, clutches were higher in woodland at Wytham than in the Botanic Garden, the difference averaging about one third of an egg. That blackbirds lay larger clutches in the country than in towns has been recorded by several observers, but others have disputed it. The data used have usually been too few to be conclusive either way. As a check on the Oxford observations I therefore analysed clutch-size according to habitat as shown on the 1955 nest-record cards. 606 clutches laid in rural habitats were available for comparison with 181 laid in urban and suburban habitats. The former averaged 3·92, the latter 3·78, a small but statistically significant difference. Though the cards from urban and suburban habitats numbered less than a quarter of the total they contained nearly half the clutches of two, while the cards from rural habitats contained all the clutches of six.

Clutch-size also varies geographically. Blackbirds lay on average slightly smaller clutches in England than they do in Belgium, Holland and Germany. The blackbirds in Shetland too, and probably also in Scandinavia, lay larger clutches than in England. On the other hand blackbirds in southern Europe and North Africa lay smaller clutches. The variation follows the same rule as in many other European birds: clutches are larger in the north than in the south, and a little larger, at corresponding latitudes, in the east than in the west.

Finally there is a source of variation in the birds themselves. Old birds tend to lay slightly larger clutches than young birds breeding for the first time. In the Botanic Garden clutches of two were laid by old and young birds about equally, but nearly all the clutches of five were laid by old birds. The clutch-size of old females averaged just over 0·4 egg more than the clutch-size of young females. In addition there were slight, but apparently consistent, differences in the size of clutch laid by individual females, irrespective of age. Thus there were two old females who laid unusually small clutches. While the other old females nearly always laid clutches of five from the end of April to late May, these two females mainly laid clutches of three and four during this period.

Thus many things go towards determining the size of a blackbird's clutch: the date on which it is laid, the weather at the time of, or shortly before, laying, the habitat, the geographical location, and finally the bird's age and other individual characteristics. It is worth while trying to see which of these sources of variation represent an adaptive response on the part of the bird to environmental conditions, and which of them are without apparent usefulness.

Seasonal variation is of greatest effect, accounting for a variation in average clutch-size of over one egg. We saw in the previous chapter that the breeding season corresponds to the period when conditions are favourable for blackbirds to raise a family. This fact immediately suggests a reason for the seasonal fluctuation in clutch-size. Conditions suitable for nesting and rearing young will not begin and end suddenly, and continue uniformly suitable from beginning to end. The beginning of the breeding season will thus be expected to be a period of gradually increasing suitability, and the end a period of gradually decreasing suitability. Just as natural selection has determined the beginning and end of the breeding season, so, with greater refinement, it could have led to the more exact fitting of the number of eggs laid at different periods of the breeding season to the birds' ability to raise young in those different periods.

There are two sources of evidence suggesting that the seasonal rise and fall in clutch-size is in fact adaptive in this way.[68] By weighing the young at the age of eight days, by which time they are of good size but not yet liable to leave the nest if disturbed, I found that the average weight of nestlings was higher in the middle of the breeding season than at the beginning and end; and this was in spite of the fact that families are largest in the middle of the season, so that each nestling must get a smaller share of the food brought to the nest than do the nestlings in the early and late nests. The second piece of evidence comes from a study of the nest-record cards. For clutches of each size, the number of young actually raised is lowest in the late nests; for the early nests the evidence is inconclusive. These facts suggest that conditions are best for rearing young in the middle of the breeding season. Probably at this time the combination of day-length, weather, and general abundance of food is at its most favourable. Days are long, though not quite at their longest, the weather is usually warm, and the flush of caterpillars and other insect larvae adds to the variety of available food. It is of special interest in this connection that while the droughts late in the breeding season, and the two droughts early in the season, all of which sealed off the worms, resulted in the

starvation of many nestling blackbirds in the Botanic Garden
and surrounding gardens, a similar severe drought in the late
May of 1956 had no serious effect on the survival of nestlings.
Families of five were successfully raised, whereas in the less
severe drought in April 1955 families of two and three were
dying in the nest. This seemed to be due entirely to the fact
that during the May drought the parents, though unable to find
worms, were able to collect quantities of caterpillars that were
falling from elm trees just outside the Botanic Garden.

The effect of weather on clutch-size seems, by contrast, to
be curiously inadaptive. Clutches are reduced below the
seasonal norm by cold weather or drought at the time of
laying, and raised above the norm by exceptionally favourable
weather, but the young from these clutches will be in the
nest two and a half to four weeks later, by which time the
weather is likely to be quite different. The birds would do
better, one might think, to remain unaffected by these temporary changes in the weather. Possibly however this response to the weather is part of the mechanism controlling
the normal seasonal rise and fall in clutch-size. Temporarily
abnormal weather may, so to speak, 'mislead' the birds and
cause them to lay a clutch which is really adapted to the
season of which such weather is characteristic. I owe this
suggestion to Dr. David Lack.

Variation according to the habitat seems to be adaptive,
though the evidence so far is scanty. Nestling blackbirds
grew better in woodland at Wytham than in the Botanic Garden, and except for those destroyed by predators very few
young died in the nest, whereas in the Botanic Garden
nestlings often died of starvation. Thus the difference in
clutch-size fitted the different feeding conditions. In this
country blackbirds seem to lay the smallest clutches of all in
city parks, where the food suitable for young birds would be

expected to be very poor. From these few facts it is reasonable to suppose that the size of the clutch is adapted to the feeding conditions in different habitats. How this adjustment comes about, whether by a direct response to the abundance of food at the time of laying, or by an ability to 'recognize' certain habitats by their appearance as, so to speak, good or bad for raising young and to modify the clutch-size accordingly, is of course unknown and would be worth investigating.

Of all the sources of variation in clutch-size, geographical variation has received the most attention. Geographical variation in the clutch-size of blackbirds is similar to that of many other European birds: clutches are larger in the north than in the south and slightly larger in the east than in the west. Lack,[41] who called attention to these trends, suggested that, other things being equal, the longer hours of daylight in the north enable the parent birds to collect more food and so feed a larger family than in the south, while in the continental east of Europe the weather is on the whole finer and insect life consequently more abundant than in the maritime west, so that larger families can be reared. Though objections can be raised in individual cases, this is still the most reasonable explanation for the main trends of geographical variation in clutch-size, and would fit what we know for the blackbird. But in addition to this it seems probable that the dry Mediterranean climate must be unfavourable for blackbirds, which depend on extracting a large proportion of the food for their young from the upper layers of the soil, so that this too would favour the laying of small clutches in the south of the range.

Finally we have to consider the differences due to age and the residue of individual variation inherent in the birds themselves. A number of species of birds are now known to lay smaller clutches in their first breeding season than later. This may be a positive adaptation, the young bird being on the whole less efficient in its first year and so, on the average, not able to raise quite such a large family as an old and experienced bird. It is a guess, but a reasonable guess when we consider how finely animals are adapted to their circumstances.

Individual differences in clutch-size are in a different category. While by their very nature they cannot be adaptive in the same way as the variations discussed above are adaptive, from another point of view they are the most important of all the sources of variation. For it is these individual differences that provide the material on which natural selection can work and so enable blackbird populations to adapt themselves to changing environments.

A further question remains: why do blackbirds never, except by an occasional freak, lay seven eggs? If the ability to feed the young were the only limiting factor we should expect that in some places, at the most favourable time of the year, clutches of seven would regularly be found. Tentatively, I suggest that here the blackbird comes up against a limit imposed on nearly all birds that build cup-shaped nests in the open, the fact that the nest will not hold more than six young. Five large young blackbirds completely fill a nest: six, which I have never seen, must overflow. Cup-shaped nests are moulded to the body of the building bird; unless the method of building is radically altered they cannot be made bigger. It can hardly be a coincidence that it is extremely rare for any bird that builds such a nest in the open to lay more than six eggs, whereas many birds that build closed nests or nest in holes have much larger clutches. For British blackbirds, however, this limit set by the size of the nest is unimportant, since the limits imposed by food and weather usually keep them well below the possible maximum: blackbirds in northern Europe, where six is a fairly frequent clutch, may have to be content with sometimes producing fewer young ones than they could feed.

—15—

Breeding Success

THERE IS a widely held belief that if a bird's nest is investigated closely, and especially if the eggs or young are handled, the parents will desert. But the danger is greatly exaggerated. Blackbirds, for instance, will usually tolerate a great deal of disturbance; so long as the contents of the nest are not permanently removed they will return to it soon after the intruder has gone. The occasional shy bird of course needs to be treated with more care: such a bird, unless the observer takes care to disturb it as little as possible, may desert its eggs, particularly during the early stages. It is exceptional for any blackbird to desert its young just because they have been examined and handled by a human being.

Blackbirds do however occasionally desert nests with eggs for no apparent reason, especially early in the breeding season when it seems that they are not yet fully in earnest about nesting and are liable to be put off by unfavourable weather or other less obvious factors. A few such desertions occurred in the Botanic Garden, but as a cause of nest failure they were numerically unimportant. One female deserted her eggs because of repeated interference by another female. The two birds, $\female 1$ and $\female 2$, had nests within about ten yards of each other. On several occasions I saw that $\female 2$, whenever she came off her own nest, immediately flew to $\female 1$'s nest and caused a disturbance. Unluckily this nest was concealed behind the thick foliage of an evergreen magnolia, so that I could not see what went on. If $\female 1$ was on the nest she was driven off: if she was not on, the intruder would spend some time at the nest, apparently interfering with it. After several days of this the harrassed $\female 1$ deserted her nest, in which the number of eggs had somehow been reduced from four to two.

Much more often, nests with eggs fall victim to predatory birds and mammals. Among the mammals, small boys are important egg-predators of suburban blackbirds in some areas. Luckily few eggs disappeared in this way in the Botanic Garden, where carrion crows were the chief enemy. Jackdaws, magpies and even jays visit the garden, the last two mainly in the early mornings, and were suspected of taking eggs, though without definite proof. The same predators attacked the nests when they contained young. I watched helplessly from the other end of the garden while a carrion crow discovered a nest in the ivy on one of the walls, clung flapping to the creeper and in a matter of seconds extracted and swallowed the young birds which had hatched a few hours previously. Crows are certainly the most feared of the visitors to the garden: time and again my attention was drawn to their presence by the high-pitched, insistent 'seee, seee' of the anxious parent blackbirds. Once I saw a magpie attack a nest and on visiting it later found that the four large young had all disappeared. Cats took a few nestlings but were not serious predators, thanks to the combined efforts of the gardeners and myself to restrict their activities. In one instance already mentioned, when a cat attacked a nestful of large young, it provided a beautiful example of the importance to the young blackbird of growing quickly and leaving the nest prematurely if disturbed. A family of four young, which I was weighing daily, had reached the age of nine days; three of them were growing well and were within 10 gm. of one another in weight, while the fourth was much lighter. When I visited them on the tenth day I found that a cat had been at the nest. It had killed and mangled three of the young, and left their corpses below the nest. There was no sign of the fourth, and largest, nestling. A few days later I found it alive and well, being fed by its parents, and it survived to independence. It had been about 5 gm. heavier than the other two well-grown nestlings, and its feathers were a little more advanced. I like to think that it owed its survival to this advantage, which enabled it to scramble or flutter out of the nest a little quicker than the others.

An unexpected predator was a rogue moorhen. In May 1956 a pair of moorhens had a nest on the small pond at the end of the garden. I occasionally saw one of them flying about the garden and perching on bushes and hedges, but thought nothing of it. On June 11th the young were just hatching in a blackbird's nest in a yew hedge about forty yards from the pond. In the morning three young had hatched and there were still two eggs; but when I visited the nest again in the afternoon I found only one nestling and one egg. Next morning I revisited the nest and found that the remaining nestling had gone; there was one egg in the nest. Hanging in the hedge a few inches from the nest was a decapitated moorhen, which had evidently been systematically visiting the nest and taking the young ones until ambushed by the gardener's cat.

Three female blackbirds in or near the Botanic Garden were killed during the night as they incubated their eggs, the morning's inspection showing nothing but a pile of feathers in and around the nest. Probably the attacker was in each case a tawny owl: it certainly was in one case, as a tawny owl feather was left lying among the blackbird feathers under the nest.

Another cause of failure was starvation. Sometimes only one or two of the smaller nestlings died and the rest flew: in other cases the whole family died one by one. The signs of starvation are not difficult to tell if the nests are visited frequently enough and one is familiar with the appearance of healthy nestlings. Starved nestlings increase in weight more and more slowly and then begin to lose weight. The development of their feathers is not however correspondingly retarded, so that at the age of eight or nine days they appear small and wizened, but with their wing-feathers sprouting. They can hold out for a few more days, but if at the age of eight days they were below about 40 gm., I found that they did not survive to fledging even if the food supply improved later.

In spite of these various hazards I found that exactly 50 per cent of the nests started in the Botanic Garden and immediate surroundings produced fledged young. Studies of other species suggest that this is an average figure for garden birds. On the other hand the blackbirds nesting in woodland at Wytham were much less successful, only 14 per cent of their nests resulting in fledged young. Predation was the cause of almost all the failures, but it was not easy to decide what predators were responsible. Most often there was no clue, the nest being simply found clean and empty or sometimes with a little wet patch at the bottom from the spilt contents of an egg. Other nests were found with the eggs either neatly holed and sucked or with the shells chewed into little bits. These last I took to be the work of small rodents. As in the Botanic Garden, sitting females were sometimes attacked. One bird which had nested almost on the ground among some brush-wood used to sit very tight on the eggs. She was the only one of the woodland birds that year which would stay on the eggs until I stood beside her and reached out my hand. Her exceptional boldness was probably her undoing: one day I found that all that remained of her was a heap of feathers round the nest.

In the Botanic Garden different pairs had widely differing degrees of success. In the course of the four years I followed 59 pairs through from the beginning of the breeding season to the end, obtaining a complete nesting history for each. Each pair reared an average of 4·1 young per year. The three most successful pairs reared 12, 11 and 10 young, each from three broods, while the 13 least successful pairs reared none at all. These figures include pairs of which one member was killed in the course of the breeding season. I found that old pairs were more successful than young pairs: excluding those pairs of which one member was lost, pairs of old birds reared an average of 6·3 young, while young pairs averaged only 3·4 young.

After leaving the nest the young are still liable to fall a prey to the same predators as take them from the nest. In the Botanic Garden carrion crows were again undoubtedly the chief of these. In addition many recently fledged blackbirds were taken by tawny owls at night. A few others apparently died of starvation at times when the weather made feeding difficult for their parents. A few died from accidents such as drowning. Nevertheless, a high percentage of the blackbirds that left the nest survived to independence. I calculated the survival in two stages, from leaving the nest until five days after, and from then until independence. 81 per cent of the fledglings survived the first five days, and of these 81 per cent again survived the next two weeks until they were independent of their parents. Thus of all those that left the nest, 66 per cent survived to independence.

Breeding has not been fully successful until the young birds form part of the next year's breeding population. The number of young produced by each pair that survive till the following breeding season is thus a much more meaningful measure of their success than the number leaving the nest or surviving to independence. Unfortunately I could not obtain this figure for the pairs in the Botanic Garden, as too many of their young moved away after they became independent and were not seen again. But another lot of birds filled the gap. Each year, as mentioned earlier, recently independent and unringed young birds came into the garden from late June onwards. Almost certainly most of these were from nests in the near vicinity, as shown by the fact that they included a few that I had ringed in nests in neighbouring gardens. I trapped and ringed some of these newcomers and was surprised to find how many of them remained in or near the garden and bred in the following year. In fact, as mentioned earlier, it became clear that very soon after they have become independent of their parents these young blackbirds choose the place where they will settle down if they survive the winter. In any case the number still present in the following breeding season gives a minimum measure of survival from the time of reaching independence until the next breeding season. I found that of 26 young birds trapped from the end of June to early August, at least 16, or 62 per cent, were alive in the following March.

We now have a set of figures that enables us to assess the

reproductive success of the Botanic Garden population. Each pair on average reared 4·1 young to the fledging stage. Of these, 66 per cent, or 2·7, reached independence; and of these, assuming that their survival was similar to that of young birds born just outside the garden, 62 per cent, or 1·7, would be expected to be alive at the beginning of the following breeding season.

——16——

The Botanic Garden Population

THE NUMBER of blackbirds present at any moment in a circumscribed area is obviously affected by many incalculable factors and may not in itself be of much significance. In autumn and early winter the number present in the Botanic Garden fluctuated markedly, depending on the visits of the numerous young birds and trespassing adults which came from outside to feed on the fruit trees. At times, as many as fifty birds might be present in the garden. In addition, the resident adults often left the garden to feed in the hedges near by. In winter, when the fruit crop was finished, the population was reduced to the adult territory-holders and a few young birds that held small, often temporary, territories. At the end of the winter, usually in February, the main influx of young birds took place, and it was at this time that most new pairs were formed and the pattern of territories was established which, with minor modifications, lasted through the breeding season and into the following winter. Clearly it is on this settled, breeding population that attention must be concentrated.

The density of the breeding pairs in the six acres of the Botanic Garden was very high, but probably not above what it is in many English gardens with abundant cover and well-tended lawns and flower-beds. In the four years of this study there were 11, 16, 13 and 13 pairs, giving an average density of nearly two to nearly three pairs per acre.

If the figures for the four years are combined, 38 per cent of the breeding birds were in their first year, but the proportion varied in the different years (Table 1). In 1954, following a year with a low breeding population, a large number of young birds settled in the garden; this was the only

TABLE 1. Proportion of old and young blackbirds in the Botanic Garden breeding population

	males		*females*	
	old	young	old	young
1953	6	5	—	—
1954	7	9	8	7
1955	10	3	10	2
1956	9	4	8	6
Total	32	21	26	15
Percent	60	40	63	37

Note: In 1953 the ages of too few females were known for inclusion. In 1954 the age of one female was unknown. In 1955 one male was unmated at the start of the breeding season. In 1956 one male was bigamous.

year in which the young males outnumbered the old males. In 1955, when a large number of old birds survived from the high population of the previous year, very few young birds settled. In 1956 the proportion of young birds was intermediate. These figures, though too few to be conclusive, suggest that the number of young birds settling each year may be greatly, or primarily, determined by the size, and survival, of the previous year's population.

Males and females were in approximately equal numbers in the established population in the four years. There were two bigamous males, but also a few males that were unmated for limited periods. But it seemed that in the surrounding area there was a slight excess of males in the adult blackbird population. Unmated young males were commonly seen until well into April. Most of those in the Botanic Garden that eventually acquired mates paired with females which had lost their mates. As has been mentioned, one male did not get a mate at all in his first breeding season. But hardly any young females were known to be unmated after the end of March. Furthermore, males that lost their mates in the course of the breeding season were less successful in re-mating than females that lost their mates. In my population, seven males lost their mates. Five of these remained unmated for the rest of the season; the other two acquired new mates, one after twenty-seven days, the other after an unknown period but not more than about sixteen days. Eight females lost their mates. Five of these moved away from their territories immediately. Two of the eight were not seen again; but the other six (three that moved away and three that stayed where they were) all acquired new mates, four of them almost at once, or as soon as they were ready to re-nest, and the other two after about twenty and thirty days.

On average, exactly two thirds of the adults survived from the beginning of one breeding season to the beginning of the next, the proportions being similar for both sexes (Table 2). Hence, if the total population had remained constant, on average a third of the breeding birds each year would have been in their first year. In fact 38 per cent were in their first year. The excess over the expected percentage was due to the unusually large number of young birds in the breeding population in 1954.

TABLE 2. Survival of adults from one breeding season to the beginning of the next

	males		females	
	Initial number alive	*Survived to next b. s.*	*Initial number alive*	*Survived to next b. s.*
1953	11	7	4	3
1954	16	11	14	8
1955	12	8	12	9
All years	39	26 (67%)	30	20 (67%)

The annual mortality in the Botanic Garden was a little lower than the average for the whole country. An earlier analysis of the recovery of ringed birds from the whole of Britain showed that on average only about 60 per cent of adult blackbirds survive from one year to the next.[38] With such a high annual mortality, only one blackbird out of about one hundred can expect to live as long as ten years. But their potential age is considerably higher: there are records of caged blackbirds living for nearly twenty years.

As we saw in a previous chapter, the Botanic Garden population produced an average of 4·1 young per pair per year to the fledging stage. Of these, it is probable that on average about 1·7 per pair survived until the next breeding season. With an annual mortality of 33 per cent, each pair needs to contribute an average of only 0·7 young to the next year's breeding population in order to replace its losses. The Botanic Garden blackbirds therefore contributed considerably more than their share of young birds to the population over these four years. As the mortality and productivity figures were similar in each year it is probable that this local population has been consistently overproducing.

If the number of young birds settling in each year is largely determined by the number of gaps left in the previous year's population by the death of old birds, as the figures suggest, and if the local population is producing more young birds than are needed to fill these gaps, and these young birds, as we have seen, do not disperse far before settling down, we should expect to find keen competition among the young males for territory space. This was indeed the case. By the end of March the earliest of the young males were beginning to breed, but many were still unestablished at this time and some did not get territories until well after the breeding season had begun. Over the four years, twenty-six young males were established in the Botanic Garden and immediate surroundings by the end of March, and seven established themselves later in the breeding season. Two of these took over territories of birds that had been poisoned, and three others replaced males that had died in other ways. The other two carved out new territories for themselves by annexing parts of the territories of their neighbours. There was also one young male living in the area that did not get a territory at all in his first year. Thus only about three quarters (26 out of 34) of the young males that settled in the garden and its immediate surroundings acquired territories by the beginning of their first breeding season, though most of the others succeeded in establishing themselves a few weeks later.

Observations in the different years provided a more detailed picture of how this competition for territories affected the individual birds. In 1953, when the breeding population was low, all the young males got their territories by the beginning of the breeding season. There were no late arrivals, and no birds that tried and failed to acquire territories. But in 1954, when the population was the highest recorded, there seemed no doubt that in early spring the territory-holding males prevented some young males from establishing themselves in the garden. Three young males sang persistently for several days from high trees, unable to establish themselves on the ground below, which was already fully occupied. Of these one later established himself in the garden when a territory fell vacant on the disappearance of a territory-holder, but the other two eventually moved away. A fourth young male, already mentioned, remained for the whole breeding season in or near the garden, but never obtained a territory in that year; in 1955 he established himself just outside the garden. In addition to these persistent males, there were other young males that made briefer appearances in the garden and tried to acquire territories, but they soon disappeared, apparently because of opposition from the territory-holders.

In March 1955 a number of territory-holders were killed by rat poison that had carelessly been left uncovered. This unfortunately disturbed the population just as breeding was about to begin, but it was valuable in showing how intense competition is for territories in a favourable area. In the course of just over two weeks, one territory was taken over by six successive males after the poisoning of the original owner. Certainly three, probably four, of the six were poisoned, upon which their places were at once taken by the next. The sequence of males was as follows:

$\male$5, original owner, an old bird. Found dead March 20th.

$\male$50, an old bird. Took over territory, having appeared in the area at the end of February. Previous history unknown. Poisoned March 27th.

$\male$14, an old bird, which in previous breeding season had territory in very urban back-gardens about 40 yards away. Took over territory on March 27th, but seen there for only one day. Probably poisoned.

Unringed young male. Took over territory on March 29th. Appeared suddenly in area; previous history unknown. Poisoned on April 2nd.

♂22, an old bird, in possession of adjacent territory. Annexed territory on April 2nd. Poisoned on April 3rd.

♂52, a young bird, who had been trying since January to establish himself in the garden and had acquired a small territory about 40 yards away, which he occupied intermittently. Took over territory on April 3rd.

♂28, a young bird, which had been trapped as a juvenile in the garden in the previous summer and had been present in the vicinity all autumn and winter without acquiring a territory. Took over territory on April 4th, pushing back ♂52 towards the area previously occupied by ♂22.

In 1956 there were three young males that established themselves well after the breeding season had begun. Two of these took over pre-existing territories on the death of the previous owners, while the third carved out for itself a very small territory at the junction of three other territories.

Unfortunately most of the young males that tried, and failed, to establish themselves in the Botanic Garden were unringed, so I could not find out where and when they eventually established themselves. The only one that was ringed was ♂19, the male that did not obtain a territory until his second year and settled just outside the garden. I think that probably most of those that failed had to be content with less suitable territories in more open parkland near by. One young colour-ringed male, which on March 25th, 1955 was singing hard, so probably trying to establish himself, in a well-populated area on the edge of Magdalen Meadow, about 500 yards from the Botanic Garden, later moved 700 yards and established himself in a row of hawthorns on the edge of a playing field, a similar habitat but with less cover. Here he settled and bred in two successive years.

As already mentioned, a third of the adults died each year. These deaths were not spread out evenly through the year. Very few established adults died in the five months from the end of June to the beginning of December. This proved to be easily the safest time of the year: out of 54 established colour-ringed birds alive at the end of June, 52 were alive at the beginning of the following December. Nor were the three winters, all of which were hard or very hard, responsible for many deaths, 46 (87 per cent) having survived out of the 53 established colour-ringed birds living in the garden before the cold weather started. By comparison, mortality during the breeding season was rather high: 18 birds died or disappeared during the period March–June, compared with 11 in the other eight months of the year. Ten of these certainly died, as their remains were found; the other eight disappeared suddenly, although they had nests, so almost certainly died. These figures are given in full in Table 3. The birds which were poisoned in March 1955 have of course been omitted.

TABLE 3. Deaths and disappearances of adult blackbirds in the Botanic Garden

	Established birds found dead		Unknown or un-established birds found dead		Established birds disappeared	
	♂	♀	♂	♀	♂	♀
January	—	1	—	1	—	—
February	2	1	—	—	3	1
March	—	1	3	—	—	—
April	1	2	1	—	2	1
May	2	2	—	—	1	1
June	2	—	—	—	2	1
July	—	—	—	—	1	—
August	—	—	—	—	—	—
September	—	—	—	—	—	—
October	—	—	—	—	—	—
November	—	—	—	—	1	—
December	—	2	—	—	—	—

In a few cases I was able to determine the cause of death. Of the twenty-one birds (omitting those that were poisoned) found dead in the garden, five were killed by tawny owls, and three by some other predator; two were found with a broken or dislocated neck, probably having flown into some obstruction, one was killed by a motor vehicle, one was killed by a school boy, and one was probably killed in a fight with another bird. For the other eight there was no visible cause of death. These make up about one half of the adult birds dying in the area: the other half must certainly include a much higher proportion of birds taken by predators.

I saw many violent fights between blackbirds, especially in early spring, and one bird was found dead in the Botanic Garden with injuries that appeared to have been inflicted in a fight. Dr A. D. Blest watched one female killing another in a garden near the Botanic Garden in March 1954, and I have found altogether more than ten reliable accounts of fights between blackbirds leading to death. Many more fights must lead to injuries which later contribute to death. Fighting may thus be a commoner cause of death in blackbirds than it appears to be in most other species of birds: it is presumably commonest in densely populated suburban habitats, where competition for territories and mates is fiercest.

Deaths of blackbirds reported through the British Trust for Ornithology ringing scheme are distributed in the same way as those in the Botanic Garden. Most of them, naturally, are reported from garden habitats. Table 4 shows the months in which 348 birds, ringed as nestlings in Great Britain, were found dead in subsequent years; 55 per cent of them died in the four-month period March–June. It has often been assumed that most small birds die in winter, and that mortality during the breeding season is comparatively light. This is probably true for many species, but it may be doubted

TABLE 4. Month of death of 348 adult blackbirds ringed as nestlings in Great Britain

	Found dead in second calendar year of life	Found dead in later years
January	26	17
February	25	15
March	25	19
April	36	27
May	32	18
June	20	15
July	21	9
August	10	8
September	3	4
October	3	3
November	4	1
December	4	3

whether it is typical for the common birds living in urban and suburban habitats. In close agreement with the blackbird figures, Summers-Smith[74] found that 54 per cent of house sparrow deaths occurred in the breeding season (April–July). He suggested that the high mortality during this period is due to increased predation and to the physical effort of rearing successive broods, while mortality in winter is low because in suburbia food is readily available and birds do not incur the risks of migration. For the blackbird the same explanation probably accounts for the low mortality in winter. During the breeding season it may be suggested that the birds are more vulnerable, not only to predation, but to hazards of all sorts, because of their preoccupation with nesting duties.

In addition, it is probable that the more crowded the breeding population is, the more likely each bird is to succumb to one of the many possible causes of death. I cannot demonstrate this point statistically from the present study, but a single instance may be given in illustration. In 1954 an old pair, ♂7 and ♀7, had their territory much constricted by the establishment of a young pair, of which the male, ♂21, was an exceptionally aggressive bird. ♀7 had previously foraged in the Botanic Garden, but eventually their reduced territory hardly contained any suitable feeding ground, and when feeding her second brood in 1954 she habitually flew across the High Street to a neutral feeding area in a field on the other side. On May 27th she collided with a bus when flying across the road with food for her young and was killed.

We now have some of the key facts relating to the number of blackbirds in the Botanic Garden. They may be summarized as follows:

The breeding population is very dense, and has produced more young than are needed to replace its losses.

More young birds have tried to take up territories in the garden than have succeeded in doing so. The number of young birds that have been able to settle each year seems to have depended mainly on how many old birds survived from the previous breeding season.

Not more than three-quarters of the young males in the area have acquired territories by the beginning of the breeding season.

More birds have died in the breeding season than at any other time of year. Mortality during the autumn and winter has been light, although the winters were hard.

The causes of death, as far as they can be determined, have been mostly predation, with accidents probably second in importance. Fighting may cause some deaths at the beginning of the breeding season and may increase liability to death from other causes.

These facts strongly suggest that in a favourable habitat like the Botanic Garden, territorial behaviour limits the breeding density, at least locally, by preventing some birds from settling in the area which they would otherwise have chosen. In this context, 'territorial behaviour' must include both the aggressive behaviour of established birds and the tendency for newcomers to move elsewhere when they meet more than a certain amount of opposition.

The density which is thus reached is not however determined solely by the behaviour of the birds; it depends also on the cover. Where cover is thick, so that neighbouring birds are more effectively hidden from each other, a denser population is possible. Thus in the Botanic Garden there has been a tendency for territories to be smallest along part of the northern wall, where trees, groups of bushes, the gardener's house, and the wall itself, effectively reduce visibility far below what it is in the rest of the garden. This effect of cover is, I think, largely responsible for the very sparse breeding populations of blackbirds in open habitats, even where nest-sites are abundant and the food-supply good.

If the total number of blackbirds in the Oxford area is to stay more or less steady, some local populations must contribute fewer young birds than are needed to replace their losses, to balance the surplus produced in very favourable breeding habitats such as the Botanic Garden. Other local populations may be in an approximately balanced state. In general, numbers in the less favourable habitats must be continually recruited from the more favourable. The total number of blackbirds over a wide area must be determined by a complex process of local over-production, local under-production, and movement from one habitat to another. We have not yet nearly enough data to enable us to see how this process works, but the little information available for other local populations will take us a few steps forward.

—17—

Other Populations

EACH YEAR at the beginning of the breeding season I made a census of the male blackbirds holding territories in the University Parks, an area of about seventy acres half a mile from the Botanic Garden. Although there were only two colour-ringed birds among them in the four years, both born in the Botanic Garden, it was comparatively easy to make an accurate census. Established males are very sedentary at this time and are continually occupied in defending their territories, and territorial patrollings between neighbouring birds demarcate the borders clearly at some points. A few males had individual distinguishing marks, and in addition the first-year and old males were readily separable. In the four years, my censuses showed 31, 34, 34, and 34 males established in the University Parks at the beginning of the breeding season in late March. Although the average density was one male to just over two acres, the territories were not noticeably larger than those in the Botanic Garden, as much of the area consists of playing fields and rough grassland of which only the edges are defended.

The proportion of young birds holding territories at the beginning of the breeding season was consistently lower than in the Botanic Garden, with an average of only 23 per cent (Table 5). However, almost certainly more young birds

TABLE 5. Proportions of old and young male blackbirds in the breeding population of the University Parks

	old males	first-year males	% first-year
1953	24	7	23
1954	24	10	29
1955	29	5	15
1956	26	8	24
Total	103	30	23

established themselves each year after the censuses, which were made in the last days of March. Each year at the time of the census some young males, apparently not yet established, were seen being chivvied and chased by the territory-owners, and random counts of all males seen, as opposed to the actual census of territory-holders, gave a figure of 29 per cent young males. This is still considerably lower than the percentage in the Botanic Garden.

In each year the proportion of young males in the University Parks, though consistently lower, varied in parallel with the proportion in the Botanic Garden. There were most young birds in 1954, and fewest in 1955. Though the number of years and the absolute numbers involved are too few to be conclusive, the figures suggest that in the University Parks, as in the Botanic Garden, the number of males that can settle in each year is limited by the number of old birds surviving from the previous year. Other evidence supports this suggestion. Young males would be found for several days occupying quite unsuitable territories, such as a clump of trees with no undergrowth in an open field, apparently unable to secure a more suitable piece of ground. In the most favourable parts of the park the size and distribution of the territories in the different years were very similar (Fig. 22). The occupation of marginal areas with little cover was less regular; some of these were on the edge of the park and were apparently occupied intermittently by birds the main part of whose territory was just outside the census area.

The blackbird population of the University Parks fluctuated much more in the course of the year than that of the Botanic Garden. In the Botanic Garden, as already mentioned, the population was relatively stable throughout the year, except in autumn and early winter, when visiting birds came to feed on the fruit trees, and in cold weather in winter, when many territory-holders temporarily left the garden for better feeding places. The University Parks on the other hand attracted large numbers of blackbirds all through the winter, which came to feed on the playing fields and, in December, on the fruit of the many exotic *Crataegus* trees. Most of these visitors were first-year birds. Some may have come from farther afield, but almost certainly most of them were of local origin. Few first-winter birds were to be seen in the surrounding gardens at this time. Throughout the winter I occasionally saw colour-ringed first-year birds, born in the Botanic Garden, feeding in the University Parks, and regularly saw them on other playing fields nearer the Botanic Garden.

I made a large number of random counts of the numbers of old and young males seen in various garden and park-like

L   161

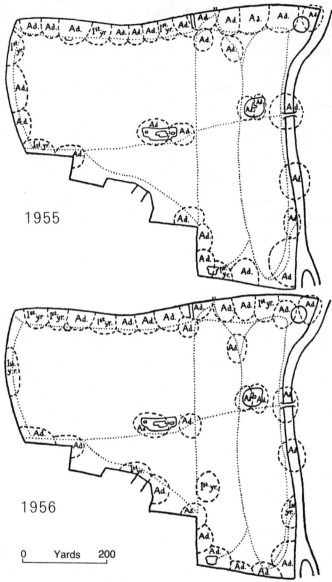

FIG. 22. *Blackbird territories in late March in the Oxford University parks.*

habitats round Oxford. These showed the same differences as were found between the University Parks and Botanic Garden (Fig. 23). The proportion of young males in parkland is higher than in gardens throughout the winter, but becomes

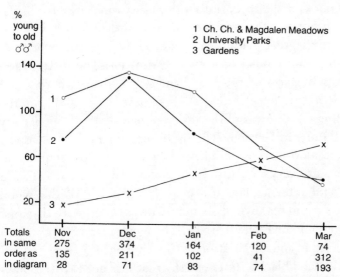

FIG. 23. *Proportions of young to old birds in Oxford gardens and parks. November–February figures based on random counts. March figures: gardens based on Botanic Garden population over four years; parks and meadows based on random counts.*

lower in the breeding season. This is due to the shift of the young males from their winter feeding grounds in open parkland to their preferred breeding habitat in gardens. The rise in the number of first-year males in gardens in early spring in any one year may be much more obvious than appears from the figure. After the end of the cold spell in February 1954, and again in 1955, young males appeared suddenly and began to establish themselves in town gardens where for the previous weeks only the resident males had been seen; and it is at this time that young males make themselves conspicuous all over the town by singing in the late afternoon from high on buildings and trees.

Information on woodland populations is harder to obtain. The winter population of woodland is sparse and more un-settled than in gardens and parkland, the birds moving in loose flocks and concentrating in places where the feeding is good. It appears that many of the old birds leave their terri-tories for a great part of the time. However, the density of the breeding population can be estimated. The distribution of nests in parts of the woodland at Wytham where I was confident that I had found all first nests suggested that the breeding density was of the order of one-tenth of the density in the Botanic Garden. This is in agreement with censuses made in an oak wood in Surrey.[8] In addition, the population appeared to vary annually, being much lower in 1956 than in 1954 and intermediate in 1955. In stretches of the wood where I could find five or six nests in 1954, not more than one or two could be found in 1956. The figures for a Surrey wood also show an annual variation of the same order.

Woodland blackbirds are so shy that it is not easy to obtain close enough views of males to be able to distinguish their age. But almost as soon as I started observations in Wytham I noticed that the males, as far as they could be seen, seemed to be predominantly old birds, and a large proportion of the females that allowed a close approach before leaving the nest were dark, probably old, birds. Eventually I determined the ages of thirty-nine males seen in the breeding season. Of these only five (13 per cent) were first-year birds.

At least in gardens and parkland, blackbirds normally main-tain their territories throughout life, once they have settled, or at most shift only short distances. It follows that, as long as numbers in a local population are fairly stable, a high pro-portion of first-year birds in a breeding population implies a high adult mortality, and a low proportion of first-year birds implies a low adult mortality. The data therefore suggest that the annual mortality of adults is higher in gardens than in parkland, and perhaps higher in parkland than in woodland. This is reasonable, as that part of the mortality—and it seems to be a considerable part—which results from the hazards of a densely crowded population will be progressively mitigated in the more sparsely populated habitats. For the woodland population, however, this conclusion is not certain from the present data, as there was evidence that the breeding population at Wytham was by no means stable over the four years of the study; nor is it certain that the adults retain their territories from year to year in woodland as they do in gardens and parkland.

Tentatively, we may contrast garden and woodland populations as follows. Gardens are densely populated, breeding success is high, and an excess of young birds is produced, which do not disperse far before they try to settle. Territorial behaviour sets a limit to the breeding density and not all young birds that try to settle are able to do so. This habitat is therefore normally saturated and the density of breeding blackbirds rather stable. Woodland on the other hand is sparsely populated, and breeding success is low. The density of the population in any year is probably dependent not on territorial behaviour but on the survival of adults over the previous winter, on the production and survival of young from the previous year, and possibly also on the number of young birds immigrating from neighbouring habitats where breeding success is higher. The breeding population is therefore not at its maximum each year, but fluctuates considerably.

However this may be, the figures that have been published for the breeding density of blackbirds in many different habitats and in several different countries (Table 6) show that the differences in density between the blackbird population in the Botanic Garden, University Parks and Wytham woodland are typical. The densest populations of blackbirds

TABLE 6. Breeding densities of blackbirds, pairs
per hectare (2·47 acres)

British Isles

Botanic Garden, Oxford	5·0–7·3
Overgrown garden, S. Wales[12]	6·7
Cotswold farm-house garden[27]	3·2
Dublin suburb[32]	1·8
University Parks, Oxford	1·2
Surrey oak wood[8]	0·2–0·7
Oxfordshire farmland[13]	0·4
S. Wales farmland[12]	0·3
Open country, Shetland[77]	0·01

Other parts of Europe

Frankfurt Park (with thick cover)[72]	2·6
City park, Zürich[18]	2·6
Parkland, Zürich[18]	2·2
Berlin suburb[72]	1·8
Urban area with small gardens, Zürich[18]	0·8
Garden city, Zürich[18]	0·6
Augsburg Zoo (parkland with sparse cover)[72]	0·3–0·5
Town and gardens, Oederan, Germany[23]	0·4
Borghese Garden, Rome[1, 23]	0·4
Oak-hornbeam wood, Germany[55]	0·3
Urban area with few gardens, Zürich[18]	0·2
Swiss orchards and fields[18]	0·2
German pine plantation[60]	0·2
Finnish mixed woods[56]	0·2
Swiss mixed wood[18]	0·1
Deciduous groves('Laubhaine'), Finland[56]	0·08
Deciduous meadow-like woodland ('Laubwiesen'), Finland[56]	0·05
Spruce and mixed coniferous woodland, Finland[56]	0·04
Marshy deciduous woodland, Germany[60]	0·015

are to be found in gardens, British gardens being more thickly populated than German and Swiss gardens, perhaps because of richer vegetation and better cover. Parkland supports fewer blackbirds than gardens, the density clearly depending mainly on the amount of cover. Farmland supports a breeding population only about one-twentieth as dense as the best gardens, doubtless partly because of the poor cover and probably also because of less good feeding conditions. Woodlands on average support a low population. The density of the blackbird population of English oak woods may, as we have seen, be about a tenth of what it is in the most favourable gardens, but other kinds of woodland mostly support much lower populations. As we shall see in the next chapter, woodland was the blackbird's ancestral habitat. Like some other birds, they now find a man-made environment more favourable.

18

Blackbirds elsewhere

BLACKBIRDS are found from the Azores, Madeira and the
Canary Islands in the west, through Europe and northwest
Africa to Russia, the mountains of central Asia, and the
northwest Himalayas. Isolated by many hundreds of miles
from these western populations they occur again in the lowlands of China. In spite of the gap in distribution Chinese
blackbirds are so similar to the others that they are generally
considered to belong to the same species. Other blackbird-
like birds occur in southern Asia, but because their plumage
is partly grey or white and they differ in other ways from
typical blackbirds, they are probably best treated as separate
species.

Among European birds the blackbird's closest relative is
the ring ouzel, which breeds in mountains well above the

blackbird's typical habitats and is completely migratory. The song, calls and habits of the two species are all rather similar, the most obvious difference being the presence of the white gorget in the ring ouzel. The two species are almost completely isolated from one another during the breeding season by their different habitats, and they probably compete little, if at all; but their present preference for different habitats may have been evolved as a result of competition in the past. Even now they are intolerant of each other. Ring ouzels which come down to rest and feed on blackbird territory when on migration are sometimes persistently attacked. But even on migration contact is normally avoided, as ring ouzels prefer to come down in places which are as similar as possible to their breeding habitats.

Blackbirds were introduced into Australia and New Zealand by man about ninety years ago. Where the climate is suitably mild and humid they have done well. They have become established and widespread in parts of south-eastern Australia, and have not only spread all over the main islands of New Zealand but have colonized all the outlying islands as well, apparently unassisted by man.[79] They are now among the commonest of New Zealand birds, and the blackbird's song is as familiar a sound in the suburbs of Dunedin as it is in Oxford. In behaviour and ecology they seem, to judge from recent observations,[21] to differ little from their European cousins. They have no close relatives among the native birds of Australia and New Zealand, and the resulting absence of competition has probably contributed to their success. On Norfolk Island, one of the outlying islands which they have colonized, 450 miles northwest of New Zealand, the very similar grey-headed blackbird is also found. Dr Arthur Cain, who visited Norfolk Island in 1953, tells me that he saw both species together in the same habitat. An interesting study of interspecific competition awaits any ornithologist who may go to live on Norfolk Island. Will the two species eventually occupy separate habitats, as the blackbird and ring ouzel do in Europe?

The western blackbirds have been divided into a number of races on the basis of colour and size, but these races are only rather slightly differentiated from one another and some of the lines of demarcation are arbitrary. The birds living in the north of the range and in mountainous areas are large. In particular, the blackbirds of the northwest Himalayas are relatively huge, with a wing-length about 30 mm. greater than that of British birds. The smallest blackbirds are those living along the southern part of the western seaboard of Europe, in the lowlands of northwest Africa and in some of the Atlantic islands. As in many other species, the birds living in the coldest places tend to be the largest; but the situation needs further investigation. Wing-length, the standard measurement, is probably not an altogether reliable measure of size in the blackbird: there is some variation in the shape of the wing, and it may be that migratory races of blackbirds have relatively longer wings than the sedentary races.

Geographical variation in the colour of the plumage mainly affects the females. Females from southern Europe, north Africa and the Atlantic islands are darker and greyer than those from the north, even in their first-year plumage. In addition, birds from the south of the range, both male and female, acquire yellow beaks earlier than those from the north. Males often have yellow beaks early in their first autumn, and nearly all females have yellow beaks by their first breeding season. Thus, though the significance of this in the life of the birds is uncertain, blackbirds, like human beings, develop the appearance of full maturity earlier in the south than in the north.

Blackbirds are known to most people in this country as birds of gardens rather than woodland. They are familiar too as birds of open farmland, and on the Scottish isles they live in quite open windswept country. But originally they were shy birds of wooded country with a more or less thick undergrowth, avoiding gardens and the neighbourhood of man. Bewick (1804) describes the blackbird in Britain simply as 'a solitary bird, frequenting woods and thickets'. Later writers in the mid-nineteenth century describe it as nesting in woodland but frequenting the neighbourhood of houses and even coming into towns in winter. By the end of the nineteenth century it seems to have become as thoroughly a garden bird as it is now, but its spread into the centre of large cities has mainly taken place in the last forty years.

In other parts of Europe the colonization of gardens is even more recent and the process is probably not finished yet. Its earliest beginnings are unrecorded. In northern France, the Low Countries and central and southern Germany the regular colonization of town gardens started between 100 and 150 years ago and spread steadily. The spread of this colonization towards the north and east can be traced in some detail.[26, 36] The Elbe was reached about 1875, Denmark about 1890, Mecklenburg about 1900. East Prussia was not affected until the 1930's, but the gardens of southern Sweden were colonized about 1900, those of Norway in the early 1910's, and those of southern Finland in the early 1920's. Recent information is not available for most of Russia, but up to the last war blackbirds had not yet penetrated into the towns of the Crimea.[35] In southeast Europe the blackbird is still mainly a bird of the wooded mountains. The information for southern France and Italy is scanty, but there is some evidence that blackbirds have been garden birds in parts of Italy for considerably longer than in northern Europe. Nor do we know when blackbirds first became garden birds in north Africa. They are now common not only in the relatively fertile gardens of the north coastal strip, but also in some of the oases along the northern edge of the Sahara.

Although town gardens now supply most of a blackbird's wants, they are still often unsuitable for roosting, especially in winter when trees and bushes are leafless. Blackbirds that roost in their territories, as do most of those in the Botanic Garden, are intolerant of intruders, but when they are forced to roost away from their territories, or if they have no territories, they seek the company of other blackbirds at roosting time. Thus in winter great communal roosts may develop in woods and thickets on the outskirts of towns; reed-beds are also sometimes used.[7, 17] Such roosts are not very common or conspicuous in England, where there is usually thick cover in even the smallest gardens, but they are a conspicuous feature of some of the towns of central Europe,[6, 23] where the cover in gardens and parks is usually sparser than in England and the winter nights are much colder. At dusk hundreds of blackbirds may converge from all over the town towards some clump of spruce or other evergreen tree, dispersing again in the morning to their feeding places. These communal roosts develop each year after the breeding season and last until the following spring, when most of the territory-holders begin again to roost in their territories.

It has been possible to write of the blackbirds of the Oxford Botanic Garden without mentioning migration. I had no evidence that any of my ringed birds moved more than about two miles away, and much evidence that most of them were sedentary. But a small percentage of the blackbirds born in the south of England migrate: several have been found in Ireland in following winters, and a small number in continental Europe to the south of the British Isles. It would be interesting to know if these migrants are mainly garden birds or birds of open country and woodland. Further north, many of the blackbirds born in the north of Britain migrate to Ireland. An analysis made some years ago[39] showed that 25 per cent of the blackbirds ringed as nestlings in northern England and found dead in subsequent winters were recovered in Ireland, the other 75 per cent being found where ringed. Of blackbirds born in Scotland and the Border country, 33 per cent were found in Ireland and another 3 per cent in places to the west of their birth-place. Almost certainly, more complete data would show that the percentage of migrants in the population increases gradually from south to north. There was no evidence that young blackbirds migrate more than old: among those migrating west to Ireland, first-year individuals were no commoner than they were among those found at their birth-place.

Northern and central European blackbirds are also partial migrants, the percentage migrating probably increasing from south to north and from west to east. Norwegian and Swedish birds mostly come to the British Isles in winter, only a small proportion going south of the English Channel to winter quarters in France and the Iberian peninsula. Danish birds also come to Britain, with a rather larger proportion going south of the Channel. German and Swiss birds go south-west to France, Spain and Portugal, and some also to Italy, especially from eastern Germany. Details for the countries further east are not well known, but blackbirds occur as winter visitors in Mesopotamia and Palestine, and some cross the Mediterranean to Egypt and Libya, so probably eastern populations of blackbirds migrate in a southerly rather than a southwesterly direction. There is no marked tendency for young birds to migrate more than old, as has been found in many other birds, but more females migrate than males.[16]

German studies have shown that the migrants include birds born in both towns and woodland.

The number of blackbirds wintering in northern Europe has been increasing in recent years, a change that is probably connected with the recent amelioration of the climate and in particular with the milder winters. Theoretically it is to be supposed that local populations which are partially migratory are those for which the advantages of migrating and of remaining sedentary are nicely balanced. A slight change in climate would therefore be expected to alter the balance; and the means for rapidly altering the habits of the species are to hand, since according to whether the climate improves or deteriorates, natural selection will at once begin to favour the more sedentary or the more migratory section of the population.

That migration is often dangerous we know well, but we cannot assess the danger quantitatively and compare it with the danger of not migrating and so facing a severer winter. Sea crossings must be especially hazardous. A migrating blackbird has been seen to alight on the sea for several seconds and take off again unharmed;[10] but its alighting was due to misjudging the height of a wave: it is certainly not usual for them to rest in this way. Like many small birds, blackbirds seem to prefer to fly low over the water, at least during the day, perhaps because the wind speed is reduced near water-level.

As well as wind and waves, predatory gulls may be a menace during a sea-crossing. A blackbird was watched approaching Spurn Point in Yorkshire on an October day, flying just above the waves. Four common gulls 'swooped down over it repeatedly as if trying to force it into the water. The blackbird, however, managed to evade their attacks, reached the shore and immediately took cover in the nearest clump of sea-buckthorn'. A thrush had earlier been seen being harried by the same four gulls, and was probably forced down and eaten.[14] This habit may be not uncommon in gulls. In November 1954 I watched several gulls in the middle of the English Channel relentlessly pursuing a starling which was flying northwest towards the Kent coast. The gulls harried and swooped on the starling, which twisted and turned and was finally forced down close to the waves. The chase eventually became so distant that the starling's fate could not be seen, but its chances did not seem good.

But the dangers of migration can bring new gains as well as loss. Wind-blown stragglers from the main stream of migration were probably responsible for the original colonization of the Azores, Madeira and the Canary Islands, which are today regularly visited by stray migrants of many species. If the milder winters continue, it will not be surprising if Iceland, which often receives blackbird stragglers, is soon colonized in the same way. On the other hand the Faeroes, Shetland and many of the outlying islands north and west of Scotland were colonized after they had been visited for many previous years by regular winter visitors.[77] Some of the visitors, presumably from Scandinavia, eventually remained for the summer, bred successfully, and thus established resident populations.

NOTES ON THE OBSERVATIONS
OF OTHERS

(Chapters 4–8)

THE TERRITORY

STEINBACHER,[73] Jackson[32] and Lind[44] have published full accounts of territory in the blackbird; less complete accounts are those by Heyder,[23] Morley,[51] Steinbacher[72] and Lack and Light.[42]

Venables and Venables[77] found that in Shetland, where blackbirds are very sparsely distributed, territories in the sense of defended areas hardly seemed to exist, no doubt simply because there were few opportunities for neighbouring pairs to meet, but in all other places where blackbirds have been studied, with one exception, they have been found to maintain clearly defined territories. Steinbacher[72] claimed that in a Frankfurt park, where he considered the breeding population to be exceptionally high (2·6 pairs per hectare), no clearly defined territories were possible. His birds were not colour-marked. His account shows that there was much trespassing, that there was a great deal of formalized aggressive displaying, and that parts of the area, which were much frequented for roosting and drinking, could not be properly defended by the local residents, but it is not made absolutely clear that for most of the day the birds did not maintain definite territories. Since he attributed the lack of territory to the very dense population, which was however not nearly so high as in the

Botanic Garden where territories are strictly defined, his conclusion is open to doubt.

Jackson, apparently the only observer to have published a substantial account of a colour-ringed population followed the year round in a suburban habitat in the British Isles, found broadly the same situation as in the Botanic Garden, that territories were maintained all the year, with varying strictness, and that pairs stayed together. In most respects Jackson's observations agree with my own, but there is an apparent discrepancy over what he called 'subterritories'. He found that from November to March young birds of both sexes occupied parts of the territories of old birds, usually for short periods. These young birds were tolerated by the owners as long as they remained subservient to them, and themselves drove out other young birds. There have been instances of such subterritories in the Botanic Garden, but the status of these young birds has been more variable than Jackson's account suggests (pages 35–38). However, it is possible that many of the young birds in the winter population of the Dublin suburb described by Jackson may be migrant winter-visitors, whose behaviour may not be the same as that of the resident young birds which frequent the Oxford gardens.

In a Copenhagen suburb Lind found that some birds, either single males, single females, or pairs, occupy territories in winter, and that most of their food is found inside the territory. He found a gradual transition from birds that have no territory to those that have well-defined territories, and had no doubt that the defence of a piece of ground depends on the presence of a food supply. There seems to be a real difference here between Lind's population and the Botanic Garden birds, but the difference is not surprising. It is reasonable that on the Continent, where the winters are severe, the retention of territory in winter should be conditional on a food supply within the territory, while in this country, where territories normally afford food through the greater part of the winter, they should be maintained in all normal weather and only abandoned in the severest.

In his later observations in an Augsburg park Steinbacher found that from November onwards the blackbirds left their breeding territories and concentrated at communal feeding places, where a dominance order was established; breeding territories were not re-occupied until February or later. The situation was perhaps unusual as these fixed feeding places were kept supplied with food, so that they probably attracted birds which otherwise might have remained, at least for part of the time, in their territories.

Steinbacher's account of shifts in territory during the breeding season agrees closely with mine. He had more cases of pairs abandoning their territories after loss of the nest. From his account it seems clear that the female takes the lead in abandoning the territory, and moves away to find a new nest-site. The male follows her, and they may remain paired, but if the female moves into the sphere of influence of another male she may mate with him.

Steinbacher's observations on the relation of territory to the food supply for the young agree with my own. He found that the young were fed mainly on worms, and that these were obtained within the territory in the early part of the breeding season, but later, when the weather was dry, the territory did not afford enough food and the parents foraged on neutral ground, often a considerable distance away from the territory.

SONG AND CALLS

Heinroth[22] and others have noted that, though blackbird song starts as early as February, rather little song is heard before the first nests are started. Heinroth suggested that this was because old pairs remain together and so the males do not have to sing to attract mates, but I believe that this is erroneous for the reasons stated earlier (page 55). Several observers have noted that blackbirds begin to sing earlier in the year in towns than in country.[4, 40] Song regularly starts in London in January, and the same is true of Amsterdam.[2] In the country regular song does not begin until much later, while Oxford gardens, and probably most other suburban gardens, are intermediate. This appears to be part of the general advancement of activities connected with breeding in towns, discussed on page 129, but the difference between town and country is probably made more striking by the greater proportion of first-year males taking up territories in towns (page 163), and by the possibility that the somewhat higher temperatures in towns, and the increased noise and light, may have a direct stimulatory effect on song.

The aggressive 'seee'. Steinbacher[73] confuses this note ('ein . . . sehr leise Ruf "tiih" ') with the alarm 'seee', and does not attempt any precise interpretation of it, saying that the (combined) call seems to be given in a variety of circumstances, but especially by males in sexual mood, in the breeding season and less often in late autumn. Heyder[24] correctly distinguishes it from the alarm 'seee', but inappropriately calls it the 'Anpaarungsruf', and considers that it helps the two sexes to find one another, apparently because the female sometimes answers with the same call. Nicholson,[54] describing it as a 'drawn-out anxious "eeeee" of low volume but exceptionally high frequency', mentions its connection with aggressive behaviour, as also do Hillstead[27] and Gurr,[21] and this connection is clear, but not always explicitly stated, in other published accounts of blackbird behaviour.

Chinking. The various forms of this call (with chooking and the alarm rattle, called 'Erregungsrufe') have been dealt with at length by Heyder,[24] and discussed by Steinbacher.[73] Chinking at dawn and dusk has been investigated especially by van der Baan.[2] Van der Baan, and earlier Eygenraam,[19] noted the connection between evening chinking and ownership of territories: their observations agree entirely with my own, but the situation was different from that in the Botanic Garden, since in Holland (and in Germany) most of the chinking birds fly away to roost outside their territories (page 172). Van der Baan showed how in early spring, at the beginning of the song period, chinking at dawn and dusk gives place to song, with some transitory subsong, and she interprets song and chinking at these times as functionally equivalent.

Chooking. Heyder, in agreement with my own observations, distinguishes the 'pook' ('ein dunkles "duck" bis "pütt" ') as a variant of chooking which is associated with danger to the young from a ground predator. Heinroth and all later German writers have recognized the distinction between the warning calls against ground and flying predators.

The alarm rattle. Heyder distinguishes a special call ('Wiehern'), given by males most often just before the breeding season begins and between broods, but also occasionally in autumn. This is a chattering outburst of about eight notes 'gigigigi . . .', which he describes as remarkably similar to the alarm rattle. He notes that it is given *in vacuo*, that is, without apparent reference to the environment, but at the same time says that it seems to be a form of display, given by males in courtship mood. I cannot agree that this note, which I take to be the same as the explosive outbursts described on page 62, is especially characteristic of the circumstances mentioned by Heyder, and agree with Steinbacher, who includes it among the 'Erregungsrufe'.

The flight 'seep'. This call is recognized by most writers who have paid attention to blackbird calls. German authors, who have dealt with it most thoroughly ('Fühlungsrufe' or 'Stimmfühlungsrufe'), have stressed its function as a contact note, used during and in preparation for flight. Drost[15] and Heyder[24] make it clear that it helps to stimulate flight and to coordinate and keep contact between flying birds, being used before migratory flights and flights to roost. In the very sedentary population of the Oxford Botanic Garden this function was not specially noted, its role in territorial conflict being much more obvious. Van der Baan[2] mentions that in Holland this note is characteristic of migrant blackbirds when they visit city parks on passage and come into contact with the resident birds, and aptly likens it to 'a sort of "Excuse me" '.

THREATENING AND FIGHTING

The typical aggressive postures have been described by Lack,[43] Jackson,[31] Steinbacher[73] and Lind,[44] and less fully by other writers. The stretched neck, upward-pointing beak, fluffed body-feathers, slightly drooped wings and fanned tail are common features of most of these descriptions. Meugens[50] catches the spirit of the posture: 'Leur allure est importante et digne. Raides, ils engoncent le cou, gonflent le plumage, déploient légèrement la queue et l'abaissent de manière à toucher presque le sol.' Lack's description also is vivid: he notes that the up-stretched neck and upward pointing beak give the bird a 'curiously malevolent expression'. The effect is, I think, heightened by the partial opening of the beak and the flattening of the feathers of the side of the head, which gives a staring look to the eyes.

Steinbacher noted that in its extreme form the aggressive posture resembles the courtship posture (page 67). Because of this it is not always possible to tell from some of the less circumstantial accounts whether aggressive or sexual behaviour is being described. Steinbacher also stressed that displaying males always run and do not hop, while females, which adopt aggressive postures less readily, hop in attack. I have not been able to confirm that this is as invariable as Steinbacher says; I have seen males hop when approaching an antagonist in aggressive attitude, though more often they adopt a loping gait, half way between a run and a hop. But certainly when making the formalized runs and bows (page 69) they never hop.

Lack and Light[42] noted that in trees the attacking bird approaches its adversary in a spiral course (page 67). They also twice recorded wing-flicking by an attacking bird (page 67), and mentioned beak-snapping, which I have never seen in intraspecific encounters. Howard[29, 30] and Shanks[61] have both observed male blackbirds picking up leaves and carrying them about during aggressive displays. Lind gives a very full account of the main aggressive displays, and notes that in territorial encounters display is used only when the attacking bird has not an absolute prior advantage (page 69).

Border patrolling has often been described. Its curiously formal nature has usually been commented on, but observers do not all agree as to the exact manoeuvres, which are in fact more variable than some accounts suggest. References to communal displays have already been discussed (page 75).

Lind mentions that while the head is held high and somewhat forward in aggressive display, birds that for any reason are trying to escape notice withdraw their heads between their shoulders. Though his interpretation differs a little from mine, it is clearly the 'hunched' posture that he is describing: I can find no other reference to it. I have not found any description of what I have called the 'tail-up' posture. Jackson's and Meugens' descriptions of the typical behaviour of trespassing birds, retreating with crown-feathers raised and calling a low 'seep', are the only references that I have been able to find to this common and characteristic behaviour.

SEXUAL DISPLAYS

The male's courtship display has now been described by a number of observers, although until recently reports in the ornithological journals gave the impression that it was little-known. Most records have been of isolated observations, without details of the status of the performers: descriptions of the postures and movements involved are generally consistent with my own observations. Steinbacher[73] records the typical courtship display as a prelude to copulation, but in his description of pair-formation he mentions only chasing and other aggressive behaviour (page 88). Jackson[31] states that males court their mates throughout the first six months of the year, even if they have been mated for years. He does not make it clear whether he is referring to this display as a prelude to copulation, but his account implies not. As none of his females was colour-ringed, and his observation is contrary to my own observations on a large number of colour-ringed birds, I do not feel that his statement is convincing.

All observers agree that copulation is rather rarely seen. Heinroth[22] never saw it; Steinbacher, in his earlier study,[72] only once. Steinbacher[73] notes that copulation is initiated by the soliciting behaviour of the female, but his description of her posture is atypical, as he says that the whole head and body are held stretched horizontally. König[34] describes the typical soliciting posture. König, Littledale[45] and Heyder[25] record both birds facing each other at close quarters immediately before the male mounts, and it is suggested that the widely opened yellow beak of the male, set against the black background, acts as a 'releaser'. But the male's approach is not always from the front. Several observers have recorded that one bird, apparently the female in all cases, or occasionally perhaps both birds, may utter a succession of high-pitched twittering notes during the display. From the descriptions I cannot tell whether this is a call specific to copulatory behaviour, or is related to one of the well-known calls.

Steinbacher[73] reported that once, after a male had displayed to a female and she made no response, he went into the soliciting posture, and Geyr[20] and Rinnen[57] describe a similar posture adopted by males after copulation or between successive copulations.

A Study of Blackbirds

There has been some disagreement over the time of year when blackbirds form pairs in Britain, but little adequate observation. Statements that pairs are formed in autumn seem to be based on observations of old pairs consorting more closely together after the end of the moult, and of temporary winter pairs (page 88). Venables and Venables[77] and Jackson[32] in Britain, and Heyder,[25] Steinbacher[73] and Lind[44] on the Continent, seem to be the only writers to have based their statements on satisfactory data.

Jackson described the formation of seven pairs. All were formed in January, February or March, with the apparent exception of a pair of young birds which came together in November: but it is not made clear whether or not that they remained together until the following breeding season. Venables and Venables found that in Shetland pairs were formed in February and March.

On the Continent, where winter territories are not so general and the population is consequently not so sedentary as in this country, it seems to be the general rule for new pairs to be formed each year. Steinbacher had only one case of a pair breeding together in two successive years. Heyder and Steinbacher in Germany and Lind in Denmark all found that most pairs are formed when the breeding territories are occupied in late winter or early spring. Steinbacher stated that a few pairs were formed when the birds were still at their winter feeding places, but these feeding places were not abandoned until February or even later. Lind reported that in a few cases pairs were formed in winter, before the breeding territories were established. He mentioned 'incipient pair-formation' in mid-November, then nothing more until after mid-December at the earliest; but his account does not exclude the possibility that these autumn and early winter pairs were simply temporary associations between males and females. Heyder is the only author who specifically mentions temporary winter pairs, formed without any special display and splitting up before the breeding season begins.

Meugens and Jackson refer to the reversal of dominance between male and female once the pair is firmly established; I can find no other reference to it. Steinbacher found no evidence for dominance relationships between members of a pair.

Sauerbrei's record of courtship feeding seems to be the only authentic record of this behaviour in the blackbird.[59] Manning (personal communication) tells me that his report[47] may have been mistaken and that the supposed female could have been a large juvenile. There are, however, several records of the male bringing food to the incubating female on the nest.[23, 27, 76] Tucker,[76] discussing courtship feeding in the Turdidae, refers to its occasional occurrence in species in which it is not a normal part of courtship behaviour. Howard[30] describes how a male blackbird fed his mate at a time of excitement after a cat had made an abortive attack on their nest.

Bigamy has been reported by Kochs[33] and Steinbacher:[73] it is probably not rare. Steinbacher had not only a bigamous male, but also one which for a time had three females. The subsequent history of this quartet shows how a male can maintain only a weak hold over more than one mate when they are breeding. All three females nested. He lost one of them when he was occupied with feeding the fledged young of the earliest nester. A new male arrived and took over part of his territory, which he had no time to defend, and with it one of the females, which had just lost a brood of young and was ready to re-nest. He lost the next female when she moved fifty metres after a nest failure: a new male appeared on the scene and promptly paired with her. Thus in both cases the new male appeared just after one of the females had lost a nest. This was certainly no coincidence. It is immediately before the start of a new nest that the male attends the female most closely: the original male was unable to do this, and so was supplanted by the new males, which doubtless had been ranging widely over the area, seeking unattached females.

SCIENTIFIC NAMES OF BIRDS
MENTIONED IN THE TEXT

Blackbird	*Turdus merula*
Blackcock	*Tetrao urogallus*
Blue Tit	*Parus caeruleus*
Carrion Crow	*Corvus corone*
Chaffinch	*Fringilla coelebs*
Common Gull	*Larus canus*
Fieldfare	*Turdus pilaris*
Great Tit	*Parus major*
Grey-headed Blackbird	*Turdus poliocephalus*
Herring Gull	*Larus argentatus*
House Sparrow	*Passer domesticus*
Jackdaw	*Corvus monedula*
Jay	*Garrulus glandarius*
Magpie	*Pica pica*
Mistle Thrush	*Turdus viscivorus*
Moorhen	*Gallinula chloropus*
Redwing	*Turdus iliacus*
Ring Ouzel	*Turdus torquatus*
Robin	*Erithacus rubecula*
Song Thrush	*Turdus philomelos*
Starling	*Sturnus vulgaris*
Swift	*Apus apus*
Tawny Owl	*Strix aluco*

REFERENCES

1. ALEXANDER, H. G., 1927, 'The birds of Latium, Italy,' *Ibis*, (12) 3, 245–83.

2. BAAN, G. van der, 1953, 'Het jaarlijks verloop van het ochtend- en avondkoor van de Merel,' *De Levende Natur*, 10, 193–9.

3. BÄHRMANN, U., 1950, 'Ueber das individuelle Variieren des Gefieders der Schwarzdrossel (*Turdus merula merula* L.),' *Vogelwelt*, 71, 82–5.

4. BEDFORD, Duke of, 1945, 'The song-period of the Blackbird,' *Brit. Birds*, 38, 256.

5. BERNDT, R., 1931, 'Ineinandergeschachtelte Bruten der Amsel (*Turdus m. merula* L.),' *Orn. Monatsb.*, 39, 152.

6. BERNDT, R., 1942, 'Vom Schlafplatzflug inbesondere der Amseln und Singdrosseln (*Turdus m. merula* L. und *T. ericetorum philomelos* Brehm) in Bad Pyrmont,' *Orn. Monatsb.*, 50, 7–14.

7. BERNDT, R. and W. TAUTENHAHN, 1951, 'Ein Schlafplatz der Amsel im Schilfrohr,' *J. Orn.*, 93, 64–5.

8. BEVEN, G., 1952, 'Further observations on the bird population of an oakwood in Surrey (Eastern Wood, Bookham Common), *London Nat.*, 32, 51–77.

9. BEWICK, T., 1804, *History of British Birds*, Newcastle.

10. BILLETT, D. F., 1956, 'Blackbird alighting on the sea,' *Brit. Birds*, 49, 456.

11. BLASZYK, P., 1955, 'Gelegezahl und Neststandorttreue bei einer Amsel,' *Vogelwelt*, 76, 217–19.

12. CAMPBELL, B., 1953, 'A comparison of bird populations upon "industrial" and "rural" farmland in South Wales,' *Rep. Trans. Cardiff Nat. Soc.*, 81, 4–65.

13. CHAPMAN, W. M. M., 1939, 'The bird population on an Oxfordshire farm,' *J. Anim. Ecol.*, 8, 286–99.

14. DICKENS, R. F., 1955, 'A day of large-scale visible migration at Spurn, 27th October, 1954,' *Naturalist*, Oct.–Dec. 1955, 155–9.

15. DROST, R., 1931, 'Ueber den Einfluss des Lichtes auf den Vogelzug, inbesondere auf die Tagesaufbruchszeit,' *Proc. VII Internat. Orn. Congr.*, 340–56.

16. DROST, R., 1935, 'Ueber das Zahlverhältnis von Alter und Geschlecht auf dem Herbst- und Frühjahrzuge,' *Vogelzug*, 6, 177–82.

17. DUNSHEATH, M. H. and C. C. DONCASTER, 1941, 'Some observations on roosting birds,' *Brit. Birds*, 35, 138–48.

18. EPPRECHT, W., 1946, 'Die Verbreitung der Amsel, *Turdus m. merula* L., zur Brutzeit in Zürich, 1946,' *Orn. Beob.*, 43, 97–105.

19. EYGENRAAM, J. A., 1945, 'Het roepen der Merels in de schemering,' *Ardea*, 33, 241–50.

20. GEYR, H., Baron, 1933, 'Paarung bei *Turdus merula*,' *Orn. Monatsb.*, 41, 119.

21. GURR, L., 1954, 'A study of the Blackbird *Turdus merula* in New Zealand,' *Ibis*, 96, 225–61.

22. HEINROTH, O. and M., 1926, *Die Vögel Mitteleuropas*, Berlin.

23. HEYDER, R., 1931, 'Amselbeobachtungen,' *Mitt. Vereins Sächs. Orn.*, 3, 105–29.

24. HEYDER, R., 1950, 'Studien über Amselrufe,' *Zool. Garten (N.F.)*, 17, 242–9.

25. HEYDER, R., 1953, *Die Amsel*, Wittenberg-Lutherstadt.

26. HEYDER, R., 1955, 'Hundert Jahre Gartenamsel,' *Beitr. zur Vogelkunde*, 4, 64–81.

27. HILLSTEAD, A. F. C., 1945, *The Blackbird*, London.

28. HINDE, R. A., 1955, 'A comparative study of the courtship of certain finches (Fringillidae),' *Ibis*, 97, 706–45.

29. HOWARD, L., 1952, *Birds as Individuals*, London.

30. HOWARD, L., 1956, *Living with Birds*, London.

31. JACKSON, R. D., 1952, 'The display of the Blackbird,' *Brit. Birds*, 45, 103–4.

32. JACKSON, R. D., 1954, 'Territory and pair-formation in the Blackbird,' *Brit. Birds*, 47, 123–31.

33. KOCHS, W., 1935, 'Ein Amselhahn betreut zwei Weibchen.' *Beitr. Fortpflanzungsbiol. Vögel.*, 11, 31–2.

34. KÖNIG, D., 1938, 'Paarung der Amsel,' *Beitr. Fortpflanzungsbiol. Vögel.*, 14, 69–70.

35. KRÄTZIG, H., 1943, 'Beiträge zur Vogelkunde der Krim,' *J. Orn.*, 91, 268–85.

36. KRÜGER, C., 1940, 'Nordiske Solsorters (*Turdus m. merula*) Forekomst og Traek,' *Dansk Orn. Foren. Tidsskr.*, 34, 114–53.

37. LACK, D., 1939, 'The display of the Blackcock,' *Brit. Birds*, 32, 290–303.

38. LACK, D., 1943, 'The age of the Blackbird,' *Brit. Birds*, 36, 166–75.

39. LACK, D., 1943, 'The problem of partial migration,' *Brit. Birds*, 37, 122–30.

References

40. LACK, D., 1944, 'Earlier singing of Blackbird in towns,' *Brit. Birds*, 38, 116.

41. LACK, D., 1947, 'The significance of clutch-size,' *Ibis*, 89, 302–52.

42. LACK, D. and W. LIGHT, 1941, 'Notes on the spring territory of the Blackbird,' *Brit. Birds*, 35, 47–53.

43. LACK, H. L., 1941, 'Display in Blackbirds,' *Brit. Birds*, 35, 54–7.

44. LIND, H., 1955, 'Bidrag til Solsortens (*Turdus m. merula* L.) biologi,' *Dansk Orn. Foren. Tidsskr.*, 49, 76–113.

45. LITTLEDALE, H. E., 1944, 'Display of Blackbird,' *Brit. Birds*, 38, 36.

46. MACGILLIVRAY, W., 1837, *A History of British Birds*, London.

47. MANNING, A., 1946, 'Male Blackbird attempting to feed female,' *Brit. Birds*, 39, 26.

48. MARLER, P., 1955, 'Characteristics of some animal calls,' *Nature*, 176, 6–7.

49. MARLER, P., 1956, 'The voice of the Chaffinch and its function as a language,' *Ibis*, 98, 231–61.

50. MEUGENS, E., 1947, *La Vie des Merles*, Paris.

51. MORLEY, A., 1937, 'Some activities of resident Blackbirds in winter,' *Brit. Birds*, 31, 34–41.

52. MORRIS, D., 1954, 'The snail-eating behaviour of Thrushes and Blackbirds,' *Brit. Birds*, 47, 33-49.

53. MYRES, M. T., 1955, 'The breeding of Blackbird, Song Thrush and Mistle Thrush in Great Britain,' Part I, Breeding seasons, *Bird Study*, 2, 2–24.

54. NICHOLSON, E. M., 1951, *Birds and Men*, London.

55. NIEBUHR, O., 1948, 'Die Vogelwelt des feuchten Eichen-Hain-buchenwaldes,' *Orn. Abhand.*, 1.

56. PALMGREN, P., 1930, 'Quantitative Untersuchungen über die Vogelfauna in den Wäldern Südfinnlands,' *Acta Zool. Fennica*, 7.

57. RINNEN, H., 1951, *Gerfaut*, 41, 250.

58. ROLLIN, N., 1953, 'A note on abnormally marked Song Thrushes and Blackbirds,' *Trans. Nat. Hist. Soc. Northumb., Durham & New-castle u. T., N.S.*, 10, 183–4.

59. SAUERBREI, F., 'Amselbeobachtungen,' *Orn. Monatsschr.*, 51, 65–6.

60. SCHIERMANN, G., 1934, 'Studien über Siedlungsdichte im Brut-begebiet, II. Der brandenburgische Kiefernwald,' *J. Orn.*, 82, 455–86.

61. SHANKS, R., 1953, 'Blackbird behaviour,' *Notornis*, 5, 202–3.

62. SIMMONS, K. E. L., 1955, 'Studies on Great Crested Grebes,' Part 6, *Avic. Mag.*, 61, 294–316.

63. SMITH, A. C., 1852, 'Some further account of a Blackbird said to have become white through fright,' *Zoologist*, 10, 3665–70.

64. SNOW, D. W., 1955, 'The breeding of the Blackbird, Song Thrush and Mistle Thrush in Great Britain,' Part II, Clutch-size, *Bird Study*, 2, 72–84.

65. SNOW, D. W., 1955, 'The breeding of Blackbird, Song Thrush and Mistle Thrush in Great Britain,' Part III, Nesting success, *Bird Study*, 2, 169–78.

66. SNOW, D. W., 1955, 'The abnormal breeding of birds in the winter 1953/54,' *Brit. Birds*, 48, 120–6.

67. SNOW, D. W., 1956, 'Territory in the Blackbird *Turdus merula*,' *Ibis*, 98, 438–47.

68. SNOW, D. W., 1958, 'The breeding of the Blackbird,' *Ibis*, 100–30.

69. SOMMERFELD, E., 1930, 'Gefiederstudien an Drosseln,' *Anz. Orn. Ges. Bayern*, 2, 60–9.

70. SPENCER, K. G., 1956, 'Albinism related to age,' *Brit. Birds*, 49, 500.

71. STATON, J., 1941, 'Display in Blackbirds,' *Brit. Birds*, 35, 107.

72. STEINBACHER, G., 1941, 'Beobachtungen über das Verhalten und inbesondere über die Brutbiologie von Stadtamseln,' *Beitr. Fortpflanzungsbiol. Vögel.*, 17, 153–61.

73. STEINBACHER, G., 1953, 'Zur Biologie der Amsel (*Turdus merula* L.),' *Biol. Abhand.*, 5.

74. SUMMERS-SMITH, D., 1956, 'Mortality of the House Sparrow,' *Bird Study*, 3, 265–70.

75. TINBERGEN, N., 1952, 'On the significance of territory in the Herring Gull,' *Ibis*, 94, 158–9.

76. TUCKER, B. W., 1946, 'Courtship feeding in Thrushes and Warblers,' *Brit. Birds*, 39, 88–9.

77. VENABLES, L. S. V. and U. M., 1952, 'The Blackbird in Shetland,' *Ibis*, 94, 636–53.

78. WERTH, I., 1947, 'The tendency of Blackbird and Song-Thrush to breed in their birthplaces,' *Brit. Birds*, 40, 328–30.

79. WILLIAMS, G. R., 1953, 'The dispersal from New Zealand and Australia of some introduced European passerines,' *Ibis*, 95, 676–92.

POSTSCRIPT

FOOD AND FEEDING HABITS (CHAPTER 3)

Experiments carried out in California by F. Heppner (1965, *Condor* 67: 247–256) on the American Robin, a thrush very like the Blackbird, have proved that earthworms in lawns are detected by sight alone. Dr Heppner put his birds in small experimental aviaries floored with turf containing worms, and broadcast 'white noise' (sound with its energy distributed at all frequencies) at a level far above any noise that is made by worms in the ground. He found that his birds captured worms as efficiently when they were subjected to the noise as when it was switched off, even taking them within a foot or two of the sound source. There is no reason to suppose that the Blackbird's feeding methods are any different; but these results apply to earthworms in a lawn and not necessarily to prey moving about under leaf litter.

SONG AND CALLS (CHAPTER 5)

Since I wrote this chapter there has been an enormous increase in the study of the songs and other calls of birds, thanks mainly to the availability of reliable portable tape recorders and of the sound spectrograph (or sonagraph), a machine that produces a permanent trace of a sound (or sonagram) on special paper, with time along one axis and frequency (or pitch) along the other. By these means the development of the Blackbird's calls from chick to adult has been studied in detail by Messmer & Messmer (1956, *Z. Tierpsychol.* 13: 341–441) and the learning of song elements by Thielcke-Poltz & Thielcke (1960, *Z. Tierpsychol.* 17: 211–244). Joan Hall-Craggs (1962, *Ibis* 104: 277–299) has published a fascinating account of the development throughout one season of the song of a single male Blackbird in south Oxfordshire, in which she shows how the rather simple and repetitive song which it sang in March was gradually enriched by the formation of compound phrases of increasing complexity until the peak of elaboration was reached in May and June. From her account, and from observations that I have recently made myself, it seems probable that the contrast between the dawn song and the song heard later in the day (page 50) is in fact a constrast between the song of young males with undeveloped, repetitive songs, which sing persistently at dawn, and the song of older males, which early in the season sing mainly in the afternoon.

CARE OF THE FLEDGED YOUNG (CHAPTER 11)

In writing about the division of labour between male and female Blackbirds in feeding their fledged young, I hoped that others would investigate this interesting behaviour further. This has now been done by Phillip Edwards (1985, *Ibis* 127: 42–59), who also worked in the Oxford Botanic Garden. He found that division of the young might occur at any time from the day of fledging to about ten days later. The male usually took responsibility for all the young of early broods, but final broods were divided about equally. Other things being equal, division of the brood is advantageous, as the probability of a young bird surviving to independence decreased as the number of young that the parent in question was feeding increased. But against this, if the female fed some young from an early brood her next nesting was delayed, so that the total number of young that the pair could produce was reduced.

I now think that it was by chance that my three young males were fed by their mothers and the one young female by her father (page 108). A few years ago, in an attempt to check on this further, I colour-ringed the nestlings in a Blackbird's nest, having judged their sexes by their plumage while still in the nest (page 19), and spent as much time as I could watching them being fed by their parents after they had left the nest. One of them was fed by the parent of opposite sex, and two by the parent of the same sex.

BLACKBIRDS ELSEWHERE (CHAPTER 18)

The Blackbird has not yet colonised Iceland (page 175), but changes have been going on in northern Blackbird populations, some of which have affected the migrants that visit the British Isles in winter or pass through on migration. It has been known for about 60 years, since bird ringing in this country has been on a large scale, that Norwegian and Swedish Blackbirds winter in Britain (page 173); but it was not until 1958 that the first British-ringed Blackbirds were recovered in Finland. Between then and June 1975 there were 111 recoveries from Finland. Robert Spencer (1975, *Bird Study* 22: 177–190) has shown that almost certainly this reflects the continuing spread of Blackbirds northwards and eastwards in Europe (page 171). They were not known to breed in Finland until 1890, and were at first confined to the extreme southwest corner, having apparently colonised the country from the adjacent part of Sweden. It was not until the 1940s and 50s that they spread further east into the main part of Finland in any numbers, and it is this spread and increase that has been, as it were, monitored by the recoveries of Finnish breeding birds in Britain. At the same time more and more Blackbirds, ringed on passage in Britain, have been recovered in western France and the Iberian peninsula; but the origin of these birds is uncertain. If, as seems likely, some of them are Finnish, it must mean that the Finnish breeding population is pioneering different winter quarters from those of their parental Swedish stock, for Swedish birds winter mainly in Great Britain and Ireland. Or it may be that, in addition to the original colonisation from Sweden, the Finnish breeding population now includes birds of eastern European origin that spread up from the south. Eastern European Blackbirds are known to winter in numbers in France and Iberia. At present one can only speculate, but further ringing will probably provide the answers.

INDEX

Aggression, 44, 49, 54–6, 78
  see also display, posture
Albinism, 23, 24

Beak colour, 22, 23, 170
Blackcock, 75, 86
Breeding, at abnormal times, 129, 130
  and age of bird, 148, 164
  failures, 143, 144
  and song, 52, 54, 55
  stimulations to, 129
  survival rate, 144–6, 149, 150, 154–6
  and territory, 35, 36, 39–41, 45–8, 116, 163, 178, 179
  town *v* woodland, 128, 129, 165, 166 and weather, 125–7, 130, 131
British Trust for Ornithology, nest-record cards, 125, 133, 134, 136
  ringing scheme, 155

Calls, *aggressive 'seee'*, 58–60, 62, 64, 67, 100, 179
  alarm rattle, 62, 179, 180
  alarm 'seee', 62–4, 109, 141, 179
  chinking, 59, 60, 67, 70, 72, 101, 179, 180
  chooking, 61, 62, 95, 100, 179, 180
  flight 'seep', 63, 64, 67, 71, 110, 180
  screaming, 64, 65, 99
  of young, 109, 110
Chaffinch, 31, 32
Clutch-size, 97, 124, 125, 132, 133, 139
  and age of bird, 135, 138
  geographical differences, 134, 135, 137, 138
  seasonal variations, 132–7
Copulation, 84–6, 91, 92, 183
Courtship, during breeding season, 84
  and feeding, 91, 185
  female attitude, 84
  male display, 81–5, 182, 183
  and posturing, 67, 74, 181; in flight, 82, 83
  and song, 67

Crow, Carrion, 63, 141, 144

Display, 44
  aggressive, 69, 70, 75, 83, 176, 182
  communal, 75–7, 182
  distraction, 101
  threat, 57
  visual, 55–7

Egg, incubation, 97, 98, 101
  infertile, 57, 86, 92
  laying, 86, 97, 124–8
  see also clutch-size
Eye-rim colour, 22, 23

Feeding, calls, 64
  female by male, 91, 185
  movements, 28, 111
  parental division of, 105–8
  by stealing, 31, 32
  and territory, 45, 56, 177, 178
  by young, 110, 111
  of young, 28, 29, 33, 53, 91, 98, 102–4, 110, 111, 178
Fieldfare, 31, 47
Fighting, 73, 74, 77, 79, 155
  mortal, 74, 155
  over food, 73, 77
  over territory, 73, 77, 79
Flight-chases, 32, 33, 38, 62, 113
Flight of young, 110, 112
Food, finding of, 27, 28, 111, 117
  types of, 25, 33

Grebe, 108
Gull, 174

Hawk, 24, 62, 63

Jackdaw, 141
Jay, 29, 141

Magpie, 141
Migration, 170, 172–5, 177
Mobbing, 60, 61, 64, 72
Moorhen, 142
Mortality rates, 165

Index

THE END